FOLLOWING MY SHADOW

LOLISA MARIE MONROE

©2019 Lolisa Marie Monroe

While this book is a memoir inspired by true events, it contains some fictional events and fictional characters. The story, the experiences, and the words are those of the author.

This work is self-edited and published. Comments, reviews and typos can be emailed to followingmyshadow1@gmail.com.

ISBN 978-0-692-79133-2

Front cover: Shadow & Scott tearing up an obstacle at Gladstone Equestrian Association CDE, Gladstone NJ 2007
Back cover: Scott judging at Kenya Kids Benefit Event, Hollis Equestrian Park, Hollis Maine 2017
Photos by Lolisa Marie Monroe

Special thanks for photos from:
Spencer Monroe, Robin Neinstadt, Jere Gray,
Bonnie Kreitler & Diane Monroe

Sincere thanks to:
Linda Roth, Heike Bean, Melinda Takeuchi
and my daughters:
Jackiellen & Katelin Bonney

Reviews

"It has been a pleasure to coach Scott and help him succeed in Combined Driving. Always great to see a Morgan rise to the top and jump over the pond to compete in World Championships. Scott and Shadow have always had a special relationship. He has been a dedicated student of driving and now brings his passion for driving to competitions as a Driving Official."

> *Lisa Singer*
> *9-time National Pair CD Champion*
> *8-time USET Pair Driver*
> *USET Single Driving Team Coach*
> *ADS & USEF CD Judge*
> *Driving Instructor & Trainer*

"Most competitors are really good at one phase of a combined driving event; Scott is balanced in all three phases. I am sure both of us gave the crowds lots of pleasure. To this day, I hope Scott knows I am still faster!"

> *Lawrence 'Larry' Poulin*
> *8-time National Pair CD Champion*
> *8-time USDF National Champion*
> *Grand Prix Ridden Dressage Bronze,*
> *Silver & Gold Recipient*
> *8-time USET Pairs Driver*
> *ADS & USEF CD Judge*
> *Riding & Driving Instructor & Trainer*

"Scott and Shadow are an example for all of us. They proved you do not need lots of money, social status or an expensive breed of horse/pony to compete at a high level. Scott inspired me and made me realize how much one can do if they really set their mind on a goal and work hard."

Sue Mallery
Accomplished Rider, Driver & Navigator
Senior Registered Investment Advisor

"The 'Shadow' book is a wonderful story for readers of all ages. The story is on several levels and is very meaningful to anyone who has had a special relationship with a horse. It flows from the heart and I think that's what it is all about. Heart."

Penny Nicely
ADS Senior CD Technical Delegate
Adjunct Instructor of Geology &
Geoscience Western Nevada College
BS Professional Geology
MS Geology/Paleontology

"During the Garden State CDE in 2008, Scott was assisting the US Team Coach Lisa Singer. I asked him for help with my horse and he managed to spend a few minutes with me before my dressage test. That '15 minutes with Scott Monroe' has become somewhat legendary. It gave me the basis of things to work on and how to remove some of my horse's issues."

Cicily Hajek
Lifelong Equestrian

"As the National Coordinator of an Adaptive Sports Grant through the Department of Veterans Affairs, part of my job has been to help raise awareness about para-eligible veteran involvement in the two international sports of para-dressage and para-driving.

Scott is a U. S. Marine veteran and a great advocate for the sport of para-driving, knowing the joy it has brought to him as a world-class competitor, coach, and now judge. Scott has been a key partner in this initiative, and I have had the good fortune to work with Scott Monroe on many occasions while hosting adaptive/para-driving clinics at our center.

As a clinician, he is precise, thoughtful, knowledgeable and very encouraging to his students. He really sets them up for success and has a big heart for the horse's achievement as well. Scott has a growth mindset and applies that to his own, every-day continual learning and discovery."

Sarah Armentrout
Head of School
Carlisle Academy Integrative Equine Therapy & Sports
USEF Para-Equestrian Center of Excellence
USOC Paralympic Sport Club
PATH International Accredited Riding Center

"This is a wonderful book, besides being a compelling tale in itself, it is chock full of information, everything from how to gain a horses' trust to how to equip them for flying overseas. A must-read for every horse lover!"

Melinda Takeuchi
Professor, East Asian Languages & Cultures,
Stanford University
Lifelong Equestrian & Contributing Writer for
Driving Digest & The Whip

"I first saw Scott driving Shadow was at the Shady Oaks Combined Driving Event, in Lodi California. They were competing in the cones phase of the event and what I remember most is the obvious focus and intensity on both their faces. They were moving at high speed, through tight turns and tricky approaches, and it was obvious they were working as a true team.

My next encounters with Scott were in 2013 and 2014, when we were co-instructing at Can-Drive, a large driving clinic held in the British Columbia Rockies. I was impressed with how easily Scott made "newbie" drivers feel at ease and how well he was able to tailor his instruction to the level an individual student needed. He was a team player, supportive of the other instructors, and determined, as we all were, to make the camp as fun and safe as possible for everyone. During the camp, the clinicians were able to spend time together as a group and we developed friendships amongst ourselves that endure to this day.

Scott's talent as a clinician impressed me enough that for several years following the camps, I made the long trek for lessons with him. Today, I still use many of the techniques and hints he passed along to me, both in my own driving and when working with students myself.

Since then, I've competed at several events where Scott has officiated and he's proven himself to be competent and fair, whether acting as a Judge or a Technical Delegate."

> *Elisa Marocchi*
> *Equine Canada Certified Driving Coach*
> *Wildwood Farm, BC*

Dedication

The Voice in My head

Since I can remember, I have loved every animal that crossed my path. As a child I would head off to the neighbors in hopes of feeding a carrot to 'Poco,' the first horse I ever admired.

Horses are a passion that I carry with me to this day. However, I have only once in my life felt a true connection with a horse. That quiet peace where all you hear is the rhythmic footfall, all you smell is horse and leather and all you feel is the partnership created through the reins. In front of you, framed between her ears is a better world. "*You are one with the horse*," are the words that echoed in my mind. I was.

I can still see the trail lined with trees and a carpet of oak and maple leaves covering the ground. The rustle of the foliage under hooves gently trotting past. The softness of the light coming through the canopy above. A memory that I will always have in my heart and mind.

It was a trainer, Scott Monroe whose voice I heard in my head that gave me the courage and confidence to conquer the fear of my mare. More than a decade later he gave me the courage to conquer my fear of marriage.

This book is for Scott, my friend, my husband and my partner. Thank you for believing in my worth.

Table of Contents

Introduction

Scott Monroe was an Arborist from Connecticut with no previous horse experience. At forty, he decided to take up Combined Driving and soon aspired to be on the United States Equestrian Team.

This book shares the adventure Scott embarks on 'Following His Shadow' for nearly twenty-three years. How his determination, focus and one amazing horse made their dreams come true.

This story is inspired by true life events with many of Scott's training methods shared throughout the pages. It is an entertaining read for all who cherish the incredible bond between people and horses.

Enjoy-

Lolisa

Chapter 1

Finding My Shadow

It all started on May 12, 1993 when Bethesda After Dark, aka 'Shadow' was born. This stunning black Morgan horse had no idea he would make history and change the lives of so many people in his lifetime...or did he?

In the fall of 1996 Scott Monroe began searching for a horse. He had a mental list of what he hoped to find and started asking people he knew to keep their eyes open for his elusive dream horse. He contacted trusted horse friends like the Ballous, Kinsellas and DuBois in hopes that they may have some suggestions. Scott knew he would find the right horse, but when?

It was a cold winter evening a few months later and Scott found himself headed to a cocktail party. He could think of many other things he should have been doing and really did not want to go. Honestly, the thought of going alone made it even worse, but as if on auto pilot he found himself there. However, he soon was enjoying the holiday festivities and talking about what else... horses! It was a Christmas party at the home of Copper & Stan Drake. Little did he know that he was about to get the best Christmas present he could have ever imagined and that his life would never be the same.

The conversation of horses went around the room several times and rested back on Scott. Copper, who already owned three Morgan horses, asked him "What is your dream horse?" He responded by describing his perfect horse being a black Morgan gelding with big bones, handsome features, good feet, sound mind, strong body, brave heart, about fifteen to fifteen-three hands with kind and gentle eyes. The hostess of the party laughed "well that's easy, your dream horse is right up in Massachusetts!"

Within a few days Scott was at a barn, where the horse, soon to be named Shadow, was stabled. He admired this handsome three-year old black Morgan gelding. Bethesda After Dark was indeed the horse he had described on the outside, but he needed to know what was on the inside. Although Shadow was being sold as a driving horse, there was no carriage or harness there to put him to. This made it difficult to see how comfortable Shadow was with driving. Scott was told he could ride him if he had a mind to and he thought this would be a good way to get a feel for the horse. Scott had hired Robin Groves, a trainer and competitor from Vermont to meet him at the barn and give her opinion of the horse. The barn manager rode Shadow first, but Robin commented that when Scott rode Shadow, he brought the horse to life. They were a natural pair and seemed to move well together. He purchased Shadow in February of 1997 for $5,500. This stunning black Morgan gelding had no white markings and a cowlick at eye level. He was perfect. Born of Wyoming Flyhawk and Dreams Kate, his lineage was as impressive as his strong face and gentle eyes.

Scott had no doubt that this was the partner he had been looking for to share many adventures with

Chapter 2

Good Beginnings

Scott's story begins in Cornwall Bridge, Connecticut in the home of Spencer and Ruth Monroe and their five children. In order from oldest to youngest there were Karen, Sue, Wendy, Spencer Jr. and the youngest, Scott. There were a few years between Scott and his siblings, just enough years to make him a bit of a bother at times. Particularly when the girls began dating. Their wise parents thought sending little Scott on their dates with them was a good way to keep things innocent and a good way to get a full report of the evening's events. Scott didn't mind at all, he got to ride in a car on his 'dates' and that was the beginning of his love for wheels. His sisters, however, did not share the desire to have a little tag-a-long as part of their social lives.

Mr. Monroe owned a small general store which offered everything from window glass to freshly cut meat. They lived in a humble home behind the store. The house still stands and now is a veterinary clinic. The store has changed over the years with different owners and has lost the charm and sense of welcome that it once had.

Mr. Monroe would get up at 4:30 a.m. seven days a week to prepare for the day and open the General Store. He always made sure he was up extra early during the winter, so he could plow the driveway and store parking lot with his Jeep Wagoneer. Then he would be off to plow driveways for some of the older people in town and was always happy with a wave or a simple thank you in payment. He made sure he was done plowing in time to drive Scott around his paper route when the winter storms made it rough for bike delivery. Then he would have the store open by at least six a.m., so he could see to it that all the kids meeting there for the school bus could wait inside to get out of the cold.

The Monroe children had a good life and there was always lots of food in the kitchen and lots of stories at the dinner table. Scott learned many lessons in his youth, one being the ability to eat anything that came home from the butcher shop which proved to be a useful lesson in life. To this day you would be hard pressed to put anything in front of him that he will not eat and be thankful for. Another trait he inherited was a keen eye for detail that he learned from his mother. Ruth was a wonderful cook and homemaker who would starch the sheets so that "the crease could cut cold butter," well that was if Scott was not eating the butter right out of the package! Ruth would say that they all "ate like it was free," especially Scott & Sue.

Scott was a handful and perhaps the reason the Monroes stopped at five. One day he stuck his head through the rails in the wooden love seat in their home. Ruth could not get his head pulled out no matter what she tried. She had to call her husband home from the store to cut one of the rails out and finally free the little rascal. Then there was the day Ruth was vacuuming and Scott was following the wand around on the floor and his hand was sucked into the vacuum head. She was sure he would lose the arm! Regardless the reason they stopped with Scott, he enjoyed being the youngest and all the special privileges that went along with his station in life.

A strong work ethic and appreciation for Family, God and Country was bestowed on the Monroe children, as well as a strong commitment to the community. Mr. Monroe was the 2nd Selectman or more affectionately called 'Vice Mayor,' in Cornwall Bridge for over thirty years as well as an active School Board member for more than twenty years. He believed you should give back to the communities that you belong to and Scott inherited this trait as well. Mr. Monroe also hoped that his children would not have to work as hard as he did, like all of us, he wanted an easier life for them that hopefully did not start so early in the morning!

Upon graduation from Housatonic Valley Regional High School in Falls Village Connecticut, Scott followed his brother Spencer's lead and enlisted in the United States Marine Corps, 'Oorah!' A choice that would influence the man he is today, 'Once a Marine, Always a Marine'. After boot camp at Parris Island, he received special training in jungle warfare and para trooper school and was stationed for fifteen months in Okinawa awaiting deployment to Vietnam. One of his favorite memories was earning a 72-hour pass to Hong Kong. It was beautiful, and he wished he had money enough to stay in a nice place and enjoy more of the city. Before he knew it, he was in the cargo bay of a C130 heading back to Okie. Upon returning, he was once again on an LST, which is a flat-bottomed ship for carrying troops and tanks, headed for Japan. His company had orders for several weeks of cold weather training on Mt. Fuji. These maneuvers were difficult enough, but harder for this Yankee who loved the heat. One of the reasons Scott hates being cold to this day!

When his tour was nearly over, he was supposed to spend the last three months on the East Coast at Camp Lejeune, North Carolina. This would have been close to home, but due to some confusion he was stationed at Camp Pendleton, California. Not a bad place to finish one's hitch! In 1972 he received an Honorable Discharge as a Corporal, E-4.

The Marines reinforced his love of country, his attention to detail and his unceasing focus. He received expert rifleman, jump wings and good conduct, among other medals. He learned so many skills and life lessons while serving which have enhanced his life and the lives of those around him.

Fast forwarding to his relocation to Portland, Maine, he has had the opportunity to reconnect with Marines and join the Southern Maine Marine Corps League Detachment #1324. He is currently Junior Vice Commandant and has worked hard to help raise funds for the scholarships the Detachment gives to Marine Corps children. He is a member of the Honor Guard as well as the Color Guard and treasures his time with fellow Marines and the opportunity to give back to those who have served and their families.

Chapter 3

Pumpkin Head

It may have been that 1930's picture of his father racing open wheeled cars on the oval track at Cherry Park in Avon, Connecticut or maybe it was just in his genes. Whatever the reason, Scott always had a love of anything with wheels and the faster the better. When Scott and his brother Spencer were young, their father got them a go-kart to drive. It only had a lawnmower engine which couldn't get them into too much trouble, thankfully. They would race it up and down the long driveway from their home to the store. The best part was when it was nearly out of gas, they could drive it down the long drive to the Monroe General Store's gas pumps! If they waited too long, they would take turns pushing it to the store. The gas pump was out front, and they felt like royalty to just pull up and gas up their 'hot rod'.

When the boys were in their early teens, their father helped them cook up a new plan. 'Lot Car Racing' which meant racing cars in the oval track their dad helped them carve out in the 'lot' (field) next to their home. They would buy Mr. Weinmeyer's second hand cars, which were the perfect 'race cars.' Fifty dollars bought them a Plymouth three speed with a stick on the column and started years of racing. Scott's eyes will sparkle when he talks about their last lot car, a 1956 baby blue four door Ford Fairlane with an automatic transmission. Any car they could get for fifty to seventy-five dollars was added to the fleet. This was where Scott learned to drive, the driveway down to the store and that endless oval track carved in the dirt. For years after, his parents had the oval track mowed to keep the grass from taking over. I bet if you were to go there today you might find an old 'lot car' in the weeds, and possibly even 'old baby blue!'

Scott went to Cornwall Consolidated School and then to Housatonic Valley Regional High School in Falls Village, Connecticut. He ran track and played football all four years and enjoyed being Co-Captain of the Football team, when he could behave long enough to play. Seems he and some of his buddies, Dave Bosserman, Eddie Kenniston and Errett Allan decided to follow in big brother's footsteps 'collecting' pumpkins as a fall prank. Scott would not make it as a professional thief, as he used the 'Monroe General Store' delivery van for the get-a-way car! Off they went collecting pumpkins from several store fronts and delivering them all to the high school football field at night, in the 'inconspicuous' van. To make it all worse they rolled them down onto the field, making an enormous mess.

Let's just say that is was not hard to figure out 'who done it.' The coach was not amused and made them clean the whole mess up and return what pumpkins they could. Hopefully someone has photographic evidence of Scott spending a whole practice with a hollowed-out pumpkin on his head!

Chapter 4

Charlie

When Scott's Marine Corps tour was up, he started the long journey home. Since he was on the west coast instead of the east coast, he decided to get some wheels and drive home. He bought a Honda 750/4 motorcycle, the first 4-cylinder motor they made. This temporarily satisfied his need for speed.

He took Route 80 east, until he was near Colorado and dropped down to spend a few days with his friend Dave Bosserman, who was a Cadet at the Air Force Academy. Scott visited Dave just long enough to see 'Ike and Tina' in concert and share some laughs before he headed back to Route 80 and continued east. Dave was a life-long friend and their most recent visit was the toughest. Even through terminal cancer, Dave could laugh about their childhood antics. Dave had the joy of seeing his grandson and namesake, David, before he passed away last year. Dave was blessed with an amazing wife who cared for him so devotedly, thank you, Roxanne.

Getting back to the trip home, there were hours and days he would spend riding with fellow bikers on the road. Many of them were on leave from different branches of the military and were great company on the long and sometimes lonely journey. But this was unpredictable and before he knew it, they would break off to head in the direction of their own homes. It took more than two weeks to get from Camp Pendleton in California to Cornwall Bridge, Connecticut. This is a trip he would make several times in the future with horses and trailers and one day with me.

However, this time the trip was different as he arrived back in front of his father's general store with a scruffy face and a green military field jacket on a motorcycle. He was quickly greeted by a Connecticut State Trooper with an unfriendly look on his face and a few questions for the young Marine. Apparently, the police were looking for a man fitting the same description for a bank robbery that happened just hours before. Not the welcome home that Scott had imagined! Scott's father was out the front door of the Monroe's General Store in a flash. Sorting the situation out and assuring the policeman that even though Scott could get into some mischief, he certainly was not a bank robber. Soon Scott settled in at home and tried to stay away from the police.

Before long the two wheels of his Honda 750/4 motorcycle were not enough, and Scott felt as though he needed transportation more fitting the harsh New England weather. So of course, he bought a practical vehicle with the money he had saved while in the service. Well as practical as an orange 1969 Mustang Mach 1 with black stripes over the hood could be. The Mustang was the first of many sets of wheels that Scott would put to the test. He did not know then that he would find the most joy of his life on a vehicle without twin carbs and powered only by one horse's power.

It was several years later, his life would be changed forever, in Sharon, Connecticut which was only a few miles from where Scott was raised. Through mutual friends, Scott had been introduced to Charlie and Daphne Kellogg. Like with so many small towns, everyone gets to know everyone. The friendships that developed from meeting Charlie changed the course of history for many people, including Scott. It started with talking about carriages and horses at social gatherings and one thing led to another.

Charlie invited Scott to come and look at his carriage collection. That invitation led to a day that turned him from hot rods to horse power. The day his neighbor and good friend, the late Charlie

Kellogg, took him for a carriage drive with his pair of black draft cross horses he called the 'Blacks.' The two 'horsepower' enthusiasts would enjoy the swishes of the 'Blacks,' tails as they talked about so many things and trotted down the road. Scott was fascinated by this horseman's stories of World War II and how, because of his background with horses, Charlie was involved with shipping horses in and out of the war zones for the Calvary. His adventures captivated this Marine and a great appreciation and admiration grew within Scott for this amazing man. Every time Scott hears Sherman Potter on 'MASH' talk about the Calvary days or he sees a pair of beautiful 'Blacks,' he gets a lump in his throat and a twinkle in his eye thinking about Charlie.

Charlie was a great trainer of carriage driving and he and Daphne were very involved in founding the American Driving Society (ADS). The ADS became the foundation of rules and regulations for officials and drivers in the United States and it became a big part of Scott's life with horses. Charlie also wrote a book 'Driving the Horse in Harness,' which is a great book for the beginner in driving.

When asked about that first day he rode with Charlie, Scott shared "something pulled at my heart that day. Part of why I liked the tree care business was when you work with trees you can't get much closer to God. When horses came into my life, I felt even closer. Horses are the most intriguing, fascinating animals from their history to their elegance." Charlie ignited a fire that would burn in Scott from that day forward.

Thank you, Charlie.

Chapter 5

Before Shadow

Ever since his drive with Charlie, Scott had been interested in driving a pair of horses. A fact that many people would not believe after his many years of successful single horse driving. Pair driving was big in the United States by then and Lisa Singer, Larry Poulin, Tucker Johnson and Sharon Chesson were the best pair drivers in the country. The pairs were macho, flashy and fast and Scott's first driving dream was to drive a pair on the United States Equestrian Team.

Scott volunteered at driving events to watch these amazing drivers. He had the opportunity to work with organizers, officials and veterinarians and learn more about this sport that would become such a big part of his future. He was hooked.

Many of the drivers he met and respected told him that if you wanted to drive a pair you should start with one horse at a time. You needed to learn to walk before you could run. So, he began looking for a single horse to start with, and once he was further along in his training, he planned to work up to a pair. Scott started his search by asking a friend, Frank Kinsella and soon learned that Chelly Ames had a horse for sale that may be interesting to look at. Chelly was a young and talented rider that had taken up driving and lived in Connecticut. She had been competing at the intermediate level in driving and had just moved up to advanced level. Scott went to see the horse, but really had no idea what he was looking for. Chelly had a beautiful facility with dozens of stalls attached to a huge indoor arena.

The horse's name was Docile Dawn and he would soon learn that she was ANYTHING but Docile! He could see she had good conformation, was very forward and extremely strong. He went to see her three times, and during each visit he would drive her and spend a few hours getting to know her. With each visit being a couple weeks apart and being hesitant to drive away with a horse that may not be a good match, he kept going back. He remembers Chelly saying the first two times she had the horse all shampooed and groomed and the third time she just picked the dirt and hay out of the mare's hooves, guess she was tiring of this tire kicking man!

He finally stopped kicking tires and bought Docile Dawn. Looking back at the early days of his driving career, Scott wished he had known then what he knows now. He took some lessons with Chelly, as well as clinics with Bill Lower and Jamie O'Rourke. If he had met Dawn later in his career things would surely have been different.

Today, after over twenty-five years of experience Scott works with horses and teaches people to drive. Back then, the powerful mare was too much horse power for a beginner and just about all Scott did back then was hold on for dear life. He learned much from Dawn, mostly what not to do, his hands and mind were not ready for a dominant mare. There is a saying that has been used many times in our home, "don't out drive your headlights," this was exactly what Scott was doing and it all ended long before he knew better.

One fateful day, Dawn was running in her pasture and came in limping. Scott walked the field looking for anything that she could have caught her foot in and found a hoof sized hole in the ground sunk in several inches. He was not sure what made the hole, it may have been a wood chuck, but the damage was immeasurable. The veterinarian came out right away and determined that she had a torn suspensory ligament.

Dawn was treated and cared for, but within a few weeks the vet advised that at 19 years old, she would not recover from this injury. Scott made the tough decision to put her down and buried her there in Sharon on his property. He placed a huge boulder, as big as a couch next to the grave and had the date and her name, Docile Dawn air chiseled in the stone. Scott often says that if he knew then what he knows now, he could have gone far with that horse, but fate did not have it in store for them. The irony was that the year carved on the stone was 1993 and that was the same year Bethesda After Dark was born.

After that, Scott was discouraged and threw himself into volunteering wherever he could to learn to become a better horseman. He helped Chelly at the Gladstone driving event with a big gelding she was showing. The more hands on the better and with Chelly driving at advanced level, this was a good chance to experience what he was hoping to achieve. However, the show did not go well for them and he learned a valuable lesson about doing things at a show like you do them at home.

Normally Chelly drove this gelding with a breast collar, but for the presentation phase she put an elegant neck collar on him. Back then, presentation was a separate phase of a competition. Your turnout, which includes harness, carriage, clothing, grooming of your horse and cleanliness of your equipment were scrutinized for a separate score. The horse was not used to wearing the neck collar and moved a bit different than normal and the judges declared him lame. Chelly eventually went to the University of Tennessee and became a veterinarian, a great reminder of all the different ways you can be involved with horses. A lesson Scott learned over the next 25 years!

The next trial in his horse career was the pair of Arabians, or what Scott calls, "the start of my pair future....and the end of my pair future." After the Arabians the only pairs or pears he wants are from fruit stands or engines. This adventure started when his search led him to Gayle Reynolds, who had a pair of Arabian ponies that she was willing to lease. Scott went to see them, and they were quite a duo. One was 13 hands and the other 14.2, they did not match at all. The only match they had was that they were both geldings and were 8 years old. Scott thought with a one-year lease of the ponies, harness and carriage he would have a good idea if they would work out and he was not stuck with them if it did not. He built a separate run in shed and installed another hydrant and kept them in their own pasture. He would learn that Nazime "Nazie" was the sane one and Yasie was the crazy one!

Unfortunately...it took him a while to find out this lesson. He started by driving them separately and would take Yasie to Green Mountain Horse Association (GMHA) in Woodstock Vermont for lessons with Robin Groves. It was a four-hour drive from his home in Sharon for a one-hour lesson, so he would stay overnight in Vermont. The next morning, he would take a second lesson and then load up the horse and carriage and drive home. During one of the sessions there with Robin, Scott was driving back across the field into a small dip that lead to a shallow water crossing. Robin stepped on the carriage and Yasie went ballistic. The pony managed to get one leg over a shaft and then took off like a rocket. Robin jumped off and the speed only increased with less cargo. Now in a dead gallop, Scott started to turn the explosive pony in circles, preventing him from returning to the barn and sure disaster. He knew this would probably mean the carriage would flip over but he kept cutting the circles tighter and tighter. There were many stalls of horses and riders, some grooming their horse in cross ties and this train wreck could have hurt others, so Scott continued to circle. Eventually the carriage turned over, and the pony was flat on his side on the ground. Scott laid across Yasie's neck and head to keep him still until others could get the pony unhooked from the carriage which was no longer shiny side up. The veterinarian was soon on the scene and luckily Yazie only had some miner leg abrasions.

Scott was bruised but not broken. He called Gayle to tell her about the crash and she immediately asked him "what did you do wrong?" Funny how things turn out sometimes, he soon learned that the ponies had run away at a show with Gayle and she apparently did not think that was important information for Scott to have in his toolbox.

Once others found out about the runaway, they commented that Scott was a brave man to drive 'that crazy pair.' Too bad people could not have told him sooner! Scott would tell people where he got the ponies and they would ask if they were the ones Gayle had all the trouble with. Lisa Singer was one person who did speak up, during a lesson she told Scott that they were not a good pair, they did not work together, and they would never go anywhere. Gayle denied any issues with them. This English teacher should have spent more time telling him the truth then correcting the way he pronounced the pony's names. Only one way to pronounce 'crazy!'

He wished someone had warned him earlier, but he was thankful no one was hurt and soon ended his relationship with these Arabian ponies and their owner. Perhaps a 'pair' of horses were not in his future. Another important lesson Scott learned, there were many holes in their training, and he was lucky to have lived through it. There was no enjoyment in just wanting to get back to the barn alive.

Chapter 6

KISS

Keep It Simple Scott. The simplest things can sometime be the best training. One skill that so many horse people take for granted is the ability for your horse to just stand. No big deal, right? Wrong. Learning the art of standing was a game they would play in the barn. The game started when Shadow would have an eye on the grassy lawn and how good it would feel and taste. The goal was to roll, shake and eat. Well that was Shadow's goal. Scott's goal was to have this horse stand with no cross ties attached until he would say 'finished' and then the horse was free to go play.

Occasionally after grooming, Scott would turn away to get the harness, only to hear Shadow trotting out the door heading to the grass. Trying not to laugh, Scott would go to get Shadow and return the prodigal child to his standing position. When the training session was over for the day, Scott would remove the harness and bathe him and Shadow would look forward to the word 'finished.'

Scott could always gauge how tired Shadow was by the manner he headed to the lawn. Some days it would be at a fast trot and quick roll, chomping as much of the short grass he could get and making sure the other horses saw him getting special treatment. Some days it would be a slow walk with a lazy roll and a chomp...chomp with no care to show off his prize. No matter the type of exit, it was always a scene that Scott enjoyed and remembers to this day.

Two of the basic practices that built this amazing driving horse are long lines and round-pen work.

Long lines are simply that, a set of long webbed straps or rope lines that attach to the bridle and run through a surcingle. A surcingle is basically a strap that wraps around the midsection of the horse with rings attached at various heights between the belly and the backbone. Once the lines are through the surcingle rings they extend on either side of the horse and eventually to your hands.

They are quite long so that you can stand several yards from the horse to control his movements. It is like a dance. An opportunity to pay close attention to the horse's feet and movements as though you were learning the steps to the 'cha-cha' or a box step waltz. Watching where the horse's feet land with just the aid of the long line resting on his hind quarter. Teaching him to step over and under to change directions. It could almost be set to music. An incredible way to teach a horse to move with the lightest contact, but also a way to study movements and learn to dance with your four-legged partner. So much work can be done on the ground to prepare for driving and to test reactions to circumstances that can happen in a carriage. If you cannot control a situation on the ground, you are in big trouble when hitched. If your horse knows you are in control and trusts you will protect and guide him on the ground, then you have a great foundation to build your driving program.

The round pen is another of Scott's favorite tools for training and one he recommends to everyone he works with. If you are not familiar with a round pen, it is several sections of metal fence that you hook together to form a round pen. It makes a safe and controlled area to train a horse with the soft flow of the circle to work a horse by changing directions and gaits. By positioning his body in the proper place in relationship to the horse's body, Scott can control the movement and direction of the horse just as the Alpha mare does to the herd in the field. Then by adding single voice commands and hand signals he can change Shadow's gait and turn in circles without any contact. When you truly control the horse's feet you control the horse's mind. Every horse is looking for direction and leadership, this is one of Scott's methods to build that relationship.

Scott often tells his clients, when trying to accomplish or perfect a rhythmic working trot, a collected trot or an extended trot, to "hear it, see it, feel it." If you don't, fix it so you do. It's a partnership and you should treat it as such. Like a dance, it takes two.

Round pen work or 'working at liberty' sharpened Scott's ability to focus on the horse. That's an asset when driving an obstacle at speed. Timing has to be exact to get the needed response from your horse. This is just as important for a pleasure driver, to build that focus and understanding with your horse. Things can happen so quickly and being aware and in control is critical. Scott tries to instill this idea with all his clients. Horses live for the moment and they want to be free of fear because that is the way they have survived for thousands of years. You need to give them a safe environment and train them to look to you as the alpha horse who will take care of them. However, the role of alpha horse or herd boss carries a lot of responsibility. That is one of the reasons a good foundation, basic manners and trust need to be established and reinforced every day.

Scott has honed his training skills in the past several years and most recently achieved Professional Association of Therapeutic Horsemanship International (PATH) Level 2 Therapeutic Driving Instructor Certification. His goal is to work with more Para-Drivers (disabled athletes) and combined with his military background, work with wounded servicemen and women.

Chapter 7

Think like a Horse

The partnership and bond that Scott and Shadow forged these early years started a phenomenal chain of success working up through training level to preliminary level to advanced level and then on to Federation Equestre Internationale (FEI) which is world level driving.

This team was not easy to build, and Scott believes there are no shortcuts to any place worth going. He would spend years training and learning as he went. This incredible driving career started with riding, perhaps another gift from his dad. A man whose horses were named Thunder and Lightning! Like father, like son.

Riding can be used for conditioning a horse and keeping them in shape when driving is difficult or not available. Riding is also useful to understand how a horse balances himself during gait transitions and turns. The subtle weight shifts, and placement of feet can aid in knowing how to use reins to allow and guide the horse instead of correcting and steering him. This 'feeling' of where and how to place his feet is even more important when you are NOT on his back, but behind him in a carriage. No seat or legs to control the horse's movements, only your hands, your 'feel.' This is where Scott's "hands become the horse's feet." By controlling a horse's feet, you control his mind, his body and his balance. When working a horse, balance means safety. When a horse does not feel 'safe' or 'balanced,' it brings back their age-old fear of falling and becoming prey.

Learning from other trainers was a real help, Tom, Buck, John, Mark and his favorite Peter Campbell. These natural horsemen continued to prepare this dynamic duo for their future in driving and then in training others. Scott jokes about how these iconic horse trainers have forgotten more than he will ever know. Dedication and patience are lessons he learned and will never forgot.

There are genuine horse whisperers out there who can work with a horse for twenty minutes and change their attitude. Perhaps by just giving the horse an Alpha to follow and reinforcing that presence. Horses are herd animals and need to know who is in charge. What is so important is the follow up and continued leadership in this chain of command. Scott has learned that he can work with a horse and show improvement, but it is very important to work with the person and teach them how to continue this work and establish themselves as the herd boss. Being a herd boss isn't making your horse submissive. No one wants to submit. It's 'thinking like a horse.' People reason, horses associate. Scott believes you should think like a horse in your training, simplify each movement, each request. Patience is truly a virtue in training horses. The soft feel or give we want our horses to learn must start deep within ourselves. Only then, will the horse recognize their best interest is your only concern. Take your time, read the horse and set them up for success. Make the horse think it was his idea.

Many people considering driving may think that a couple lessons are all that is necessary to hitch up and go. One of the reasons Scott and Shadow have been so successful is the amount of time that they spent preparing and the continuation of a training routine.

Chapter 8

TPR & Pudding

Scott had started Shadow's conditioning gradually from day one, not unlike how he would prepare himself for a physically demanding sport. If Scott reached his limit in any given exercise, he knew it. Scott knew when his heart was pounding to its limit or when his wind was not enough to carry him another mile. But what was Shadow feeling, was he truly exhausted, or did he have more to offer before he met his fitness envelope?

Scott had begun volunteering at combined driving events, to help and to learn. He often got the opportunity to work in the 'Vet Box,' which he really enjoyed, especially when Dr. Bernd was the onsite veterinarian. It was a great way for Scott to learn more about horse fitness and general health issues, this would add more to his tool box and his training.

Horses needed to be evaluated after the walk section of a marathon before they start Section B. They have a ten-minute rest period and have their vitals checked by the attending vet. If they are not fit and vitals are not within the acceptable limits they will be eliminated from the remaining portion of the competition. This is for the protection and well-being of the horse.

During the evaluations Scott noticed a few of the horses coming in had vitals that were very low and showed no signs of stress. When the competition was over, Scott would find these drivers and ask their secrets. He was surprised to hear many of them also rode their horses in Competitive Trail Events. This is long distances riding over all kinds of terrain with distanced of up to fifty miles. The goal was simply to be the first one to cross the finish line with a healthy and sound mount under them. No easy task.

Each of these riders referred to a heart monitor as their best friend. Soon it would be Scott's. Mich, his veterinarian, had other clients that used monitors and she strongly recommended its use. Considering his goals in competition as well his desire for Shadow to be as fit and healthy as possible, this seemed a great way to accomplish both.

Recovery time for a horse is one of the most important things to understand when conditioning. You first need to establish what your horse's normal or base line is. Shadow's was a temperature of 99.7, pulse rate of 28 bpm (beats per minute) and respiration of 8 breaths per minute, this was his TPR. There is much information on line and vital cards you can print or perhaps ask your veterinarian for. It is good to have a list of normal TPR's on all your equine posted and easy to find. Then if there is a problem you can quickly reference this for an attending veterinarian.

Attaching the heart monitor was easy enough, one sensor would go under the saddle and one on the inside of the girth. An electrical signal would be sent from one sensor to the other, passing through the heart and receiving the beats per minute. The numerical count would be sent to a small gauge that you could mount on the dash of your carriage, now you would really know how your horse was doing, the guess work was gone. Another very important lesson that Scott discovered over their years of training was that the heart monitor was also an 'early warning device' for sickness or stress in Shadow. When they were hitched and ready to go, if Shadow's heart rate was not normal, Scott knew something was going on and Shadow needed rest or perhaps medical treatment. This was usually a signal that something was not right, and helped to diagnose Shadow had Lyme disease twice. Catching this early made a big difference in his recovery time.

Standing in the aisle of the barn, Shadow's pulse was 28 and when he was 'put to' the carriage, it was 34. Once he walked off while hitched was 50 and when Scott asked him for a trot, it rose to 82. Learning how long it took for his heart rate to return to 50 was the beginning of a long and extremely successful training program.

The shorter the recovery time between gaits, the fitter he was. After many months of increasing distances, at faster paces, Shadow's recovery times decreased, and he was fitter than ever. No longer would his blowing or panting with respiration over 120 breaths per minute mean that he was exhausted. It was often him trying to alleviate core heat, especially on 3-H (hazy, hot and humid) days! With the use of the heart monitor, Scott now knew that his heart rate was decreasing, and the panting was just Shadow's cooling system working. They would not return home as they had in the past but continue walking and letting the internal air conditioner do its job.

Knowing Shadow's heart rate at all times, made conditioning and stressing him easier and much safer. By watching his side, Scott was able to get a good idea of how rapid his breathing was and match it to his heart rate. Another way to safely build his strength and endurance. Now Scott had a real power horse in front of or under him.

Taking a horse temperature can and should be done from only one position, while stationary and to the side of his hind quarters. Holding his tail up and to the side with your feet firmly planted on the ground. Do not think every horse willingly lets you take their rectal temperature. This too, like everything else, must be introduced properly to the horse. You need to train them to accept it wherever and whenever from anybody. If you were to be so rude as not get the horse's permission to do so, you'll only be doing it once!

Much like Scott's own physical training, he never pushed too hard or too fast which would cause soreness and lack of desire to do more the next time. It was a gradual journey that they would both benefit from at each and every competition for years to come. Of course, Shadow's reason for pushing his envelope to the max was not just to win, but he knew he would be earning more food. Hay in front of him at all times and more grain laced with Platinum Performance, another game changer for Scott and Shadow. For over twenty years now, three heaping tablespoons in Scott's granola and two heaping scoops in Shadow's grain, sometimes with a pear on top.

Scott and Shadow worked hard and in all types of weather, it did not matter how hot, cold or rainy it was. Scott relied on the heart monitor and it was an indispensable tool because they had to train when they could, when Scott could steal time away from his tree care business. So, chances were the weather was bad. If he had to send his crew home because of extreme heat or pouring rain, what a perfect time to train. If the pair could work and train with mother nature stressing them, they could surely face what a competition could throw at them.

In 2005, 2006 and 2011 the pair won the United States National Single Championship. The first driver and horse to win this title three times. In 2004 while competing in Sweden on the United States Equestrian Team, Shadow was named honorary Swedish Morgan Horse of the Year. In 2005 and 2006 Shadow was named United States Equestrian Federation (USEF) Horse of the Year. In 2006, Shadow was honored with the American Morgan Horse Association International Horse of the Year Award. Ruth would say the 'proof was in the pudding,' perhaps she wasn't talking about pudding at all.

Chapter 9

Chandler & Lisa

After years of training, Scott and Shadow learned each other's movements and cues as well as two great friends understand each other's expressions or gestures. Scott's ability to focus became stronger with each day. Timing and response become more important the faster you drive and they both share the love of speed! Scott and Shadow were an unstoppable team. Every spare minute was spent training and learning. Scott was always watching amazing drivers like Lisa Singer and Larry Poulin and taking private lessons from both of them whenever it was possible.

Another of Scott's early mentors was the late Chandler Irwin. Once Scott moved up to Advanced Level driving, he and Chandler became fast friends, on and off the course. Chandler was considered one of the best single drivers in all three phases of competition. Scott was in awe of his speed in the marathon, he thought if he can do it, I can do it. Thus, the rivalry of these two great friends started. Chandler liked Shadow and said he would mature into a star someday.

His daughter Suzie was his navigator, and a good one! Only thing was, she would coach him throughout the marathon course and Chandler would keep saying "I know the way, I know the way!" She was the ultimate back seat driver. The two would entertain spectators throughout the competition. It was normally quiet when a competitor enters an obstacle, but it would be especially quiet when Team Irwin entered. People would crane their necks to hear the two banter as they were setting the fastest time of the day. There would always be something to tease them about when they all gathered for Saturday night dinner after the marathon. One particular evening, Scott made a comment that he was not happy with his dish. Chandler quietly got up, picked up Scott's plate and walked directly to the kitchen. Apparently, this man with many talents, was also a restaurateur. A few minutes later he returned from the kitchen, fresh plate in hand and his new friend the chef in tow. Always a gentleman, a serious competitor, a true friend who always put his horse first. A lesson Scott has never forgotten and a friend that will remain in his heart forever.

Like a sponge Scott wanted to soak in every experience and learn from it, and he did. From the books he still has on the shelf from Heike Bean and Charlie Kellogg to the years of traveling to clinics to take part in them or to audit. For two years he navigated for Kathleen Fallon for the opportunity to learn more about how the horse moves from another perspective. This was a great way to feel how the carriage reacts to the terrain and to the positioning of the 'gator' on the back. But surely the biggest influence on his driving career has always been Lisa Singer.

Lisa has been a mentor and friend since the beginning of his career in driving. He would load harness, hay and his Shadow in the trailer and head off on another six-hour drive to Chadds Ford, Pennsylvania, for lessons with Lisa. She has a calm yet commanding presence and complete understanding of the horse and the sport.

She has given numerous tips and suggestions, including the small scale she would use to demonstrate the one-pound rule. This is a method, not unlike a rein board. You use it to gauge the weight or pressure you are putting on the mouth of the horse through the reins which contact the bit. You ask kindly, remembering that you are controlling this horse by his mouth and respecting that contact and appreciating the connection.

The thought of a 'pound' of contact stuck in Scott's mind and he tried to think of an easy way to keep it in mind when he drove. His mother was English, perfect! An English Pound would be the ticket. For years, Scott carried an English Pound in his pocket, reaching his hand in his jacket and holding the coin as a reminder how light the contact can be to achieve controlled freedom. It is no wonder that Shadow was always so happy, for he knew that an English Pound only weights a little over a half pound.

Chapter 10

Ups & Downs

Scott thought of every possible training tool that he and Shadow could try. Scott had seen an article showing a horse- sized old-fashioned teeter totter. You remember them from the playground of your elementary school. It brought back memories of a childhood friend who had one in his back yard. Scott had struggled with this foolish balancing toy and perhaps felt the need to conquer it for himself as well as for Shadow. The benefits it could grant them in balance and trust were enormous. Scott designed the basic structure he wanted and had a carpenter build it. The rolling base was an 8" x 8" beam, 4 feet long. He had all the edges rasped off so that it was rounded and would roll back and forth. The frame of the teetering surface was made with 4" by 4" posts and was twelve feet long and four feet wide and covered with 2" by 8" planks. It was built with pressure treated wood as Scott knew he would always have it outside and wanted it to last. It was heavy, but like the cows, he could move it around with the forks on his tractor.

As with all his training, Scott broke this down into smaller pieces and built on each step. First, he led Shadow out to investigate this new contraption and give it a good sniff and inspection. Always better the devil you know than the one you don't. After the initial inspection, Scott led Shadow up and down the teeter several times, which at first felt like walking up the ramp into the trailer. Another day Shadow reached the center where the balance would shift, Scott was right there to reassure him that things were alright and off the other side they slowly walked.

In time, Scott would slowly ride up to the teeter totter and have Shadow walk up and down and eventually backup and back down the teeter under saddle. Scott saw this as a tool to build trust while pushing the envelope for both of them. Before long, they would learn to walk up the planks and stop at the top when both ends came off the ground. Standing there inching back and forth as needed to find that point of 'Zen' when they both feel like one, floating off the ground but close to the earth. The two played this game often and perhaps they both found it entertaining and enjoyed the trust they had in each other.

This was similar to the team building exercise or goofy commercials you often see, where one person just falls backwards. Trusting that a partner will be there with arms out to catch you and slowly ease you to the ground. This is the bond that Shadow and Scott had, that complete trust and expectation of safety that every horse wants to find.

Some of their experiences may be more colorful than others, like the fields of flowers they discovered. There were many great neighbors near Scott's home in Sharon and he had good relationships with them. He had a finish mower on his tractor and would mow paths around many of the adjoining landowner's fields. In exchange they would let him use the trails to drive or ride Shadow. These paths would be so wide and well-maintained that it would encourage the owners to use them for walking trails in spring, summer and fall and for cross country skiing in the winter.

Scott and Shadow loved to head out for drives and explore the world together. On one gorgeous summer day they were off for a ride as they had done so many times before and they entered a field of 20 acres in size and high with grass and full of wild flowers. Like a vision from a movie, there were Daisies, Black Eyed Susan, Goldenrod and Indian Paint all set in a backdrop of varying hues of green grasses. Off they rode without a care. Just reveling in the colors and smells of the intoxicating land they had discovered. Rows of flowers parted to allow passage and the pair galloped as if they were in slow motion. Perhaps like the field of Poppies that Dorothy fell victim to, this too was a beckoning siren that drew them in. They tossed all rules to the wind. These companions did not care, they rode on at great speed across the uncut fields relishing the afternoon together. Scott enjoyed sharing this experience with Shadow but wished to share it with others, now he has that chance.

Perhaps more people shared these special moments than Scott had realized at the time. A nearby home was for sale and the realtor was showing the property to a couple from New York City when Scott rode by. Unbeknownst to him, a deal was made that day because these week-enders saw this rogue rider galloping through the field of flowers. Scott did not know they were part of the 'staging' of the sale. Shadow should have received a commission!

Chapter 11

Secret Santa

After his discharge from the Marine Corps in 1972, his desire to be outdoors and work with nature, landscaping and trees brought him back to Connecticut. Perhaps another gift given to him by his father, who planted so many trees and roses for Ruth.

He started working for a company that was involved with landscaping and excavation. From there, his interest and focus turned to tree care and he started Monroe Tree Company. As an Arborist, he and his crew serviced trees on many of the area estates. For thirty-four years he and his team took great pride in their work.

In the early 80's he was very involved with the restoration project of the Statue of Liberty and Ellis Island. Scott took his crew and equipment to volunteer twice. They were part of a large national group of volunteer arborists caring for the neglected trees. It was a near and dear project for Scott as his grandparents came through Ellis Island so many years before.

Another of his favorite tree projects was putting the lights on the sixty-foot Spruce tree on the Town Green in Sharon and being the one to throw the switch to kick off the Christmas Season. Christmas memories would not be complete without including the year he was 'Secret Santa.' A friend just a short distance from his home was planning a large Christmas gathering and asked Scott for a special favor. Would he and Shadow dress up and drive across the front field with a sleigh full of presents for all the family and friends. Of course, Scott said yes. They gave him a Santa costume to wear. Then he went to a few stores and managed to find a blinking red nose that had a long elastic band that was big enough to go around Shadow's head.

The night of the party the duo headed out in full holiday regalia. Santa with a full white beard and Rudolf pulling the sleigh complete with a 'blinking' red nose. Shadow was not even phased by the ostentatious display. Horses cannot see what is directly in front of them, so perhaps he did not realize his nose was flashing or perhaps he was just as excited as Scott to see wide eyed children in awe as they watched Santa approach across the dark snow-drifted field.

They arrived and brought amazement to fifty or sixty people of all ages. Everyone with a smiling face, even the older guests had a look of belief in old Kris Kringle as they heard the soft 'Ho, Ho, Ho,' gentle jingles of the bells and the 'swoosh' of the sleigh runners in the snow. The pretty packages were passed around and excitement filled the cold winter air.

Once the party guests had all seen Santa, said hello to Rudolf and received their gifts, the jolly gent called to his 'reindeer' and they headed back down the field and out of sight. Perhaps the eggnog or just the holiday spirit in the air, but some even believed they saw the sleigh take to the air and fly away. When Scott arrived back in his barn and climbed out of the sleigh to take the harness off his trusted friend and pardon him from the flashing nose, he realized his sleigh was not empty at all! It had been loaded with bottles of champagne, gin, wine and whiskey. Apparently, they wanted to send some of the party home for all the elves. Well that kept the elves happy for a long time to come.

Chapter 12

Batter Up

When Scott found Shadow, he already had a dream in mind. 'Driving for America' was on his agenda. This was a hefty goal for someone who had no horse experience until age forty. He knew it would take a great deal of time and commitment. Somehow with Shadow as his partner, he realized there were no limits to what they could achieve. Within a few years they had conquered Training and Preliminary divisions and were moving up to the Advanced level by 2000. Team Shadow was a force to be reckoned with and the sky was the limit.

Perhaps we can blame Shadow for Scott's love of the New York Yankees. He would spend hours in the barn at night doing chores, cleaning harness and preparing what he needed for the next competition. He always had the radio on and would often listen to the Yankee's station.

Here he is listening to the game and puttering around the barn. Listening to the horses chew on their grain and hay. Smelling the horses and leather tack a heavenly fragrance. A relaxing environment that comforts all the senses and erases the stress and pressure of the day. A connection that many of you have felt or will hopefully feel in the future...the reward is unmatched.

On this particularly hot Connecticut night, he was updating Shadow's workout schedule for the week, listening to the Yankees of course and the munching of hay. He had a phone appointment a little later and had mixed feelings about it. A good friend had told him about her experience with a horse communicator, Linda Rawleigh. Apparently, Linda can talk to you on the phone and have a conversation with your horse, dog or cat at the same time. The thought intrigued Scott and he wondered if this was possible. He believed in the Apostles and Disciples. Perhaps there were people who could communicate on another level. He would talk to his animals often and was sure they understood him, but if this really worked, he was interested.

He had been working with Shadow for a few years but there were a few holes in their training. There were some parts of Shadow's behavior that he did not understand, and it would be helpful to find out more about his past. How he had been treated, what he was afraid of and why. The partnership he was building with Shadow was very important to him and perhaps this could help improve that. Since the first day, Shadow would not allow his hind feet to be touched. There were surely some bad experiences in his past and knowing more about what caused his fear would help Scott work with him to overcome it.

So, he made an appointment to talk with Linda for thirty minutes and made a list of questions to have her ask Shadow. She must have quite a business, because he had to book the appointment a month ahead of time, just for a half hour. When the time came, he dialed the phone, anxious to see how this would go. He wondered if he should have booked a longer appointment to ask about more than one animal.

Linda had a very pleasant voice and after quick introductions, she asked the name of the animal Scott wanted her to communicate with. He said Bethesda After Dark and she quickly asked what name he called him. She asked Scott to wait a minute as she contacted Shadow. Then it happened. Scott could hear her talking to Shadow, asking him where he was. Then she muttered a few "ahuh... ahuh... ahuh...." She returned to her conversation with Scott and said, "I am sorry, Shadow has passed."

Scott was speechless and replied that it was not possible, what did she mean by passed? She said, "He has passed on, but he is happy and surrounded by light." "Shadow is hovering around you and loves you." She continued, "He sleeps in a golden place with lots of soft straw."

Again, Scott insisted she had to be wrong and when the shock passed, he got up from his desk. From his office nook in the barn he walked over to where Shadow's stall was. A sense of relief came over Scott, almost as big as the relief on Shadow's face! Scott just stood there speechless, smiling with relief and perhaps a bit embarrassed that he was paying $125 dollars for this call!

He composed himself and asked Linda if there is any way she was talking to the wrong horse, she paused and then continued her conversation with Bethesda After Dark, aka Shadow. So now it became a game with Scott. He proceeded to ask when Shadow had passed, and was he alone when it happened? How did it happen? Linda asked the questions of 'her' Shadow and after several "ahuh...ahuh...ahuh," she replied, "he passed away about four months ago, he had been very ill, and his lungs hurt." "He was alone when he passed on and he liked to be alone and he is in no pain now and he loves you Scott."

Well that clinched it, Shadow was standing in front of him, eating 'like it was free' and glancing occasionally at him with those big soft eyes as if to say, "well she is right about the fact that I love you...but you know I hate straw!"

Scott had heard enough about 'Shadow' and decided with the remaining few minutes to ask about some of his other critters. He asked about Brea the miniature donkey, soon to find out it was not the same Brea either. Linda's donkey stood on the top of the pile of hay and would not let the others eat, a bit of a bully. She had trouble with her teeth and had to eat very slow and like 'her Shadow' also loved Scott. Well, he hoped at least the last part was right. He walked over to Brea, who was eating as fast as she could in hope for more and was afraid of 'her own shadow.' The veterinarian had just floated her teeth and given her a clean bill of health.

Then Scott asked about Teton, the nephew of his Shadow. Scott had given him to a woman in Vermont who was a small animal veterinarian with several horses. She was a good rider and could manage this needy juvenile delinquent. As Linda started to talk with Teton, Scott was surprised to hear he was a loner and he 'carried' his new owner carefully as she does not know how to use her legs to stay on his back. What a good boy? It was a relief when the time was up, and Scott could go back to his chores and 'talking' to his equine friends. Even more appreciative of all those in the barn. Back to the Yankees and catching up on the game.

Who knew he would end up in Portland, the home of the Boston Red Sox farm team, the Sea Dogs. We can only hope he comes around to be a Red Sox fan in time!

Chapter 13

Happiness

Happiness is a state of mind, a place we all must find on our own. It is not something that can be purchased or given to you by another. However, this happiness may include a person, animal, object or place. For Scott, it was cantering Shadow through acres of fields and trails near his home. He would leave all his worries behind and head out on his one-horse power muscle car (carriage) with Sandy on the back and follow Shadow. He found great joy and companionship with this stunning black Morgan. They trusted each other completely and there was nothing Shadow would not do for Scott, and in turn there was nothing Scott would not do for Shadow.

The two had an interesting relationship with Sandy as well. You see 'Sandy' was two seventy-pound bags of sand that Scott would strap on the back step of his carriage for ballast. They never went anywhere without Sandy. She simulated a person that Shadow would have to carry during a marathon, the navigator. But as with fast cars and too much horsepower, things sometimes come quicker than they should and on this beautiful day it was the edge of a stone wall. The space was always just enough to get through at a good pace, but a wheel caught the wall and tipped the carriage throwing Scott out. Sandy tried to stay on. He remembered that you never let go of the reins and held on as long as he could. After being dragged for some distance, the reins slipped from his hands. Away went his beloved horse with the tipped carriage dragging and all he could do is watch as Sandy spilled out across the field leaving a trail a blind man could follow. Shadow now startled by the unfamiliar noises and the loss of contact with Scott's hands through the reins, continued to run. Scott watched as he got further away and knew in his heart this could be the end for his great friend.

As if by divine intervention, the carriage hit a rock that righted the vehicle and the long reins dragging managed to wrap themselves around the axle, shortening the reins as one would in requesting a halt. When Scott caught up to the scene, there was Shadow looking back at the carriage as the reins had bent him to a stop. The carriage was shiny side up and Shadow was a bit startled but in good order, the same could not be said for Sandy. That day was a good reminder that happiness is fleeting and when it is in our grasp, we need to hold it and cherish it.

Chapter 14

Road to Astorp

The road to Sweden started five years before, one of the first questions he was asked by trainer Marie Borden was, "what are your goals?" Scott said, "I want to drive for the US Team." Marie laughed. When Scott's serious expression did not change and he did not return the laughter, she knew then that he was not kidding. Since then he had been preparing and now, he was ready and so was Shadow.

To be considered for the United States Driving Team you need to let the Selection Committee know that you want to be considered as a Team member. You must agree to the Code of Ethics of the organization and sign paperwork acknowledging your acceptance of the rules and costs associated with possibly traveling to Europe with the Team. As well as be willing to submit to drug testing for your horse. Once you have taken care of the necessary paperwork, you are on the radar of the Selection Committee.

Being chosen to the United States Driving Team is based on your competitive record including placement at certain selection trials. The Selection Committee considers all the candidates and selects a 'long list' of possible Team members.

Your hope is that soon you will be successful enough to be moved to the 'short list' where there can be as few as five people considered for the three-person team. There are one or two others picked as alternates. An alternate is chosen in case a member or his/her horse is unable to participate in the competition. In that case an alternate could step up and take their place.

Being an alternate is bittersweet, as you are proud to be considered worthy of representing your country, but chances are you will not be going. A Team alternate needs to continue training and be prepared to travel right up until everything is loaded on a plane at John Fitzgerald Kennedy Airport (JFK).

The deciding factor is when the Team horses have a final vet inspection the day before they are loaded in the truck to JFK. If a chosen member's horse does not pass the final horse soundness inspection, they cannot go. Or perhaps a driver is unable to compete for health or funding issues, the alternate is called. The alternate needs to be at JFK the following day with everything packed and ready to go. No small feat and little time to do it! Horse, carriages, harnesses and all the tack needed for this huge adventure loaded and ready to go. Not to mention what will happen with your business, farm and personal life while you are gone for a few weeks. An alternate is wishing the best to those on the Team but at the same time hoping for their chance to be there instead!

Prior to the final horse inspection, the host country will inform the Chefs d' Equipe if they have room for and will allow alternates to come and compete as well. Sometimes, due to the size of the event grounds, number of competitors or simple logistics, alternates are not allowed. If they are allowed, the alternate is not part of the United States Team but as an Individual representing the United States. Medals are only given to the top three competitors in two categories, Team and Individual. If an Individual 'medal's' or places in the top three, their placement does not help the Team placement, which is a shame.

Scott and Shadow found themselves in this situation in 2002 when picked as an alternate for the US Team going to Conty, France. France was not inviting alternates to complete as Individuals so the only way they would be going is by default of a Team member.

While Scott awaited any news about the possible trip, he got an interesting offer. Sue Mott was a friend and fellow driver from Canada. She with her husband Ken, had competed against Scott in the past and they wanted Scott to help them. Sue had been chosen for the Canadian Team going to France and Ken did not think he was ready to navigate for her at this level of competition. Sue had called and asked that if Scott was not needed as an alternate, would he navigate for her at this World Competition for Canada instead? He thought about her request as he waited for the call from Ed Young and news of the US Team.

The call came and Ed said the horses and drivers were all healthy and ready to go. He thanked Scott for being ready, but he was not needed this time. Disappointment soon turned into opportunity and he called Sue.

Although not with Shadow, this was a great opportunity to experience a World Level competition. It would be a great learning experience for him, from the navigator's perspective. He would be packing his suitcase after all, but not Shadow's.

This experience made him even more prepared and anxious to be on the Team in 2004. The next two years he trained even harder, he had been so close to his dream and navigating in the event made him even hungrier for it.

Chapter 15

Short List

Two months prior to the 2004 'Worlds' in Astorp, Sweden, Scott knew he was on the short list for the Team. He needed to start raising money for the trip. Flying to Europe with a horse, carriages and tack would cost about $40,000. At that time, each driver would be given about $8000 from the United States Equestrian Team Foundation. This would help, but he had a long way to go. The Saratoga New York Driving Club was a help in spreading the word and raising money to cover some of the costs, thank you!

When the Team was finally announced for Astorp, Scott was on it. Now he had two weeks to get everything ready to go. This trip to Sweden would be a once in a lifetime experience (or so he thought) and would create memories that would be treasured for years to come.

Scott had hired Judge Manning Horse Transportation. Judge lived in Sharon, had a great reputation and made trips several times a week to

JFK. At 0800 the horse hauling van was ready to go. In a beautiful dark blue Kenworth cab was Scott and Billy, the driver. Scott's smile as bright as the shining aluminum body carrying Shadow, carriages, tack and all the supplies for the trip. A morning Scott will always remember. As they drove by the 'field of flowers,' Scott was so busy looking at the daisies and Indian paint that he did not realize what they were driving into.

As they passed the field, there beside the road were dozens of his friends and neighbors waving American flags and shouting good wishes to Team Shadow. There in the middle of the crowd, was Ruth. She would always say, "Life is an adventure," and this would truly be an adventure!

Scott was bubbling with excitement and Billy the driver kept him entertained on the two-and-a-half-hour drive. The horses were supposed to be there at 1100 for quarantine. Scott had wished they could have gone back home and left one more time so he could once again see all the neighbors and friends that had gathered to wave their well wishes to him and Shadow.

Traffic was not bad, and they arrived at the animal holding center at JFK at 1030. The facility was an aging block building long overdue for rehab or demolition. The long single-story structure received

90

all animals of any type to be flown abroad that cannot be carried to your seat on a passenger plane. Though the compound was dreary and located in a warehouse area fit for a cops and robbers shoot out, the staff was the best. Despite having run this drill hundreds, maybe even thousands of times, the personnel were caring and willing to make horses and humans as comfortable as possible. The horses are all held in quarantine before boarding. There are only two places you can ship horses out of the US, here at JFK or out of LAX in California.

The Official Veterinarian for the airport goes over all the paperwork and health documents for each horse and checks vitals to be sure they are in good health. Once the horses were cleared, and all three were, they are held in quarantine for three to five hours. Then they would be allowed to be loaded on an outgoing plane.

When loading time came, a flatbed trailer holding the air boxes was driven to the stall area. A loading shoot was formed like you would imagine cattle being herded into. Each horse was led through the gate, into the air box, on the trailer. There were half wall dividers between the horses and a manger in front of them for hay and water. They were tied by a lead line in the front and the back door closed.

There was an opening two feet high at the top of the front and the back of each air box, so air could easily flow through. While moving and loading, canvas flaps were flipped down over the openings to minimize the horses seeing what was going on around them, a good thing.

Once all the horses were loaded on the trailer, Scott and the other grooms had to leave the air boxes. He watched as the trailer slowly traveled across the tarmac to the awaiting combo plane.

Passengers in the front would have no idea who was in the back of this enormous plane. For now, he was a passenger and had to get his luggage and head for security clearance. He argued at bag check about his luggage being seven pounds overweight. One hundred dollars for seven pounds over! Little did they know it was because of the peanut butter, homemade jam, Jack Daniels, seventy-five United States flags, banners, USA shirts and hats packed in with all his gear. These trinkets would be traded with or given to other competitors from around the world, a tradition started long ago. The luggage also carried the clothing he actually did need for the competition! Maybe if the woman checking in the baggage knew how important all these American trinkets were, she may have cut him some slack.

Once the luggage bill was settled, Scott headed to the TSA line for clearance. As a groom for horses, he got a special tag and a security agent escorted him to a secured entrance in the lower level of the airport. This accessed the tarmac and there was the trailer with the air boxes and Shadow.

Through a little pocket door on the side of the air box, Scott could climb back in and check on Shadow and his buddies, calming them during the loading process. As the trailer approached the plane the motion stopped briefly and then the boxes were rolled off the trailer on mechanized rollers and onto a conveyer. The conveyer then began to rise to the height of the cargo door and clanckity-clank the boxes were rolled into the large cargo bay. The noise was very loud and bewildering and the horses' eyes were as wide as saucers... so were Scott's.

Then the rumbling of the box sliding over the steel rollers faster than he thought necessary to the back of the bay. Then one final abrupt clank and it was locked into place. Scott could hear the snapping sounds as the straps were being attached and fastened and he was glad to have that part of the journey behind him and so was Shadow and company. Canvas flaps were opened, and the horses relaxed. A very impressive wall of super duty webbing was attached between them and the front wall of the bay. An extra layer of protection for any shifts because of turbulence. Scott did not want to tell the horses what was coming next! Take off.

The roar of the jet was much loader than when you are in the passenger section. The cargo bays were pressurized and air conditioned, but not insulated. The huge metal cargo bay brought back memories of the C130's in Oki. Here his job was much different from the old days. He glanced back towards the open cargo door and his mind flashed back to jump training. He could hear the cadence 'Stand up, hook up, shuffle to the door.' Not this flight!

He smiled and thought of his life-long friend Dusty Sandmeyer who was a chopper pilot in Vietnam. Dusty would tease him about his jump wings and jest "why would you want to jump out of a perfectly good aircraft?"

This flight, Scott would stay at the horses' heads during take- off and keep them forward in the box. This would prevent them from swaying back with the momentum and losing balance on their back feet. Remember that balance is safety for a horse. Mission accomplished.

Scott could stay with the horses for as long as he wanted. He would make sure they had hay and water and of course smuggled apples! It would be about nine hours to Amsterdam and between feedings and conversation he would sit with the other horse grooms in the last row of the huge combo jet. But for now, he was with his Shadow, 'following' him to Sweden. He could see that his handsome Morgan was relieved to have him there, that soft eye and "hmmmmm...hmmmmm."

Chapter 16

Midnight Ride

Shadow was next to an affectionate bay horse who took to Scott and wanted just as much attention as Shadow. On part of the flight they hit quite a bit of turbulence and Scott was uneasy and went back to check the horses. While standing in the stall, he began to feel a bit nauseous. The two reminisced about the night ride they were part of a few years ago at Steep Rock Preserve in Connecticut. It may be hard to imagine getting nauseous on the back of a horse, but please read on.

Maggie Durham, a fellow rider had invited Scott and Shadow to a late dinner and ride at a state park that had once been part of the railway system. Trains were long since gone, the tracks had been pulled and the path that remained was great for walking and riding. Part of the old train path went through a mountain. You could go back in time entering this tunnel of darkness with wetness leaking in from the top and down the sides. It was hard to imagine how this work of art had been carved or blasted within the mountain, no timbers or support beams, just sheer rock.

Scott arrived at around 6 p.m. and was amazed to see a cloth covered table with candles and wine. He may have felt a bit out of his element with the fried chicken he brought and his western saddle. Four other diners sat at the table and they talked in detail about the lineage of their horses and how accomplished each horse was in their specific discipline. Scott laughed to himself, Shadow had no specific discipline, rode, drove, cut cattle, played Rudolf, mastered the teeter toddler and gave lessons to children with Autism. The conversation centered around what they had paid for their Warmblood horses and how proud they were of them.

When dinner was over the group saddled their horses and headed out to the trail. It was pitch dark and perhaps they did not realize there would be no light until the moon was high. The hemlock trees hovering over a large section of the trail blocked out any chance of light shimmering through. Scott held his hand out in front of his face and could not see it. He remembered thinking "what the hell am I doing here!" He felt nauseous. He could not see the ground and could only feel the sudden changes of the terrain as Shadow's feet covered the uneven footing. His body swayed with the motion, wandering blindly on rocky seas. All Scott could think about is getting back to the trailers and starting the hour-long drive home.

One by one, each horse would stop at the tail of the horse in front of them unable to or perhaps afraid to pass. As each horse dropped to the back of the pack, there was Shadow, who now found himself at the front. He did not care, he just walked on and found his way leading the rest. Through the dark trees with glimpses of light here and there. Soon they reached the tunnel.

Off Shadow went, entering the two-hundred-yard long tunnel of darkness and strange smells. No fear and no hesitation, or at least if there was fear in Shadow's eyes, it was too dark to see it! Then came the series of pedestrian gates that were just wide enough to get a riding horse through. They were made of cut off steel beams that were sharp on the cut ends. If you or your horse brushed the ends of these metal monsters, there would be a serious wound. Easy enough in daylight for horse and human, but not as easy in the pitch dark. Shadow gauged his space and put them in the center of the gap. The other riders commented that they were so glad Scott had worn a bright reflective jersey so they could occasionally see him in the dark to follow. As in the true form of a 'shadow,' his horse vanished in the darkness.

Soon he reappeared as they reached the river and the moonlight reflected off the water. The horses all breathed a sigh of relief and walked into the river and drank. Honestly the riders all felt the relief as well and this was the only time on the journey they talked.

They crossed the river and reentered the wooded trail and back into the darkness. Soon they came into a camping area with several tents. The campers hearing this strange noise approaching all started shining their flashlights out of their respective tents. Aliens! Just what the horses and rattled riders needed to see, beams of light in their eyes. Scott reassured Shadow that it was not an invasion of the body snatchers and told the campers that they were just passing through and were sorry to startle them. Shadow led on finding the trail back to their starting point. When they reached the horse trailers the group decided that the whole idea of a moonlight ride sounded much better than it really was. Shadow got double treats when they got back home for being the $5500 Morgan who led the five and six figure horses through the haunted woods safely.

Chapter 17

Cute as Punch

Scott and Shadow touched down in Amsterdam and the regular passengers starting disembarking. Scott and the other grooms started preparing the horses for their departure from the cargo area. The co-pilot came to the back of the plane to tell them a Swedish Television Crew wanted to film their arrival. Since this was only the third World Singles Championship ever and the first to be held in Sweden, it seemed worthy to be seen on the evening news. Fine by the American Team, it as an honor and a little fun to boot.

Normally their arrivals were less than memorable, but not today. Scott rode in the air box with Shadow and his big bay roommate as it was slowly lowered to the ground. The TV cameras filmed the whole process. Scott told Shadow, in a small way, this was what it must be like to be a Hollywood celebrity when stepping out of the limo onto the red carpet. Shadow always was a ham for the cameras. Once all the horses were off the air boxes the rules for a brief quarantine time were relaxed so the reporters could get some news worthy quotes from the weary wide-eyed Americans. Scott did not remember the questions asked or his answers, but he did remember a lot of head nodding with a smile.

He was intoxicated by the sunny day and warm breeze that greeted them and so happy to have all six of their feet on the ground. Proud as punch to be with Shadow and representing the United States.

As soon as the hoopla was over, the horses were taken to the Animal Hotel for clearance. Scott got his baggage and headed back to get Shadow and meet his 'horse uber,' Martin Duells. He was a very kind man and Scott liked him right away. He was sure Martin was a good soul by the way his face lit up when he saw Shadow. They headed off to Astorp and the home and stables of the Asplund family.

Scott would set up training camp and would stay on the grounds to take care of Shadow. He wanted to be as close to the farm as possible which meant staying in a small camper trailer that was parked in the barn where Shadow was. There were showers in one of the other barns and a bathroom as well, so with a small bed and a fan, clean sheets and towels, he had all he needed, and most importantly, Shadow was close by. Right outside the camper were four Shetland ponies, two to a stall. The first two ponies were about five feet from the camper and every time Scott opened the door, they would be looking right at him. He described them as *'cute as punch'* and he would hear them quite often at night. A great noise to fall asleep to, the munching of hay and soft little whinnies from the cute little Shetlands. Occasionally a squeal when they would fuss at each other, but all and all they were great neighbors.

Mornings started early and there was just enough room on the floor in the camper for Scott to do his push-ups. The first 250 for him and the last 50 for the Corps. Then off to say good morning to Shadow and see to his needs.

One of the most enjoyable things of being here at the Asplund stable was the enchanting sense of family. Jan and Elsa had four charming children and they were all very involved with daily operations of the stable when studies allowed. The entire family was hard-working, kind and a pleasure to be around.

The first night Scott went into town to find a restaurant for dinner. It was a lovely surprise to see the Asplund family sitting across the room and eagerly inviting him to join them. It was so good to break bread with this family, it reminded him of growing up in the Monroe home. His whole family at the dinner table after a busy day. The way it should be.

Chapter 18

Butterflies

The first two days Scott walked Shadow a few times a day to let him stretch and adjust from the flight and so much standing. Scott was pleased to find the hay of such high quality, as some horses prefer different types and it is not good to introduce a lot of new things to a horse as their stomachs are sensitive. Platinum, the nutrient supplement that Shadow and Scott had taken for twenty years, was not available at the local tack shop. Since you could not import any type of feed or supplement, some substitutes were found, and hopefully Shadow would adjust.

On the third day they worked on dressage. Scott drove a second horse as well. It belonged to Jan & Elsa and was a good alternative. It is always a good idea to have another option, as a backup. If anything were to happen to Shadow before the event, you would need to have the alternate horse listed on the entry form or you would not be allowed to use them.

The next two days had cones on the agenda, so Scott asked if the cows could be moved out of a grassed area to set up a cones course. Jan gladly made it happen and Scott went out to check the area. He walked it for some time to make sure there were no ruts from the rain or holes made by cow's hooves in the wet ground. Such a surprise could cause a stumble which could be disastrous. Scott's mind went back to 'Docile Dawn,' and he walked the entire area again. The next day he spent three hours hauling out cones and setting up an advanced level course. From the overall length of the course to the distance between cones and the allowed time for this level, a competition quality cones course.

Interesting the time that it takes to prepare, he likened it to someone preparing a huge meal for a family. Hours shopping for the ingredients and preparing it in the kitchen. Twenty minutes at the table and the meal is over. Here he was spending three hours setting up an advanced level cones course to practice for this competition. Preparing Shadow, warming up for thirty minutes and then off to the field of cones. Two minutes and thirty-one seconds, double clear and practice is over.

For those of you unfamiliar with a cones course, the cones look almost like traffic cones, usually orange and are slanted on one side. They have a hole in the top where you place a plastic ball, or a tennis ball or even at some shows.... oranges! You design a pattern to drive through each set of the cones placed a certain distance apart. The distance depends upon the level which you are competing. Training level drivers have an opening between the cones 35 cm wider than their carriage. Whereas the advanced level drivers, only have an opening 20 cm wider than their carriage, which is less than eight inches for all the non-metric types. They are traveled through as fast as you can go. Definitely challenging and exciting to do as well as to watch.

There are usually twenty sets of numbered cones to go through and you cannot go through a set of cones out of order. If you hit a cone and knock down a ball you are given three penalty points. At the end, if you have not knocked down any balls and made it under the time allotted, you are double clear. If more than one competitor finishes double clear, there can be a timed drive off.

Every detail of the upcoming competition was flooding into Scott's head. So many things to be prepared for and the dream of going home with a medal weighed heavy on him. As he drove away from the cones course with Shadow, he followed one of the dirt roads that checkered this beautiful countryside. One road led to another and soon he found what he needed to see, a 'field of flowers.' This was not a field he would gallop through whole-heartedly with his trusted steed. It was just for looking at. Tulips and daffodils littered the massive grassy expanse. The flowers seemed to be dancing in the air, above the green stems and blossoms. As they stood in amazement of this mirage, he realized that it was butterflies! There were so many and of so many colors that they seemed like extensions of the colorful blossoms. So thick was the kaleidoscope of winged 'flowers,' that it was difficult to see the space between the petals and the wings. As he soaked in this gift of nature, he noticed Shadow was also staring into the field, his soft eye and that "hmmmm...hmmmm...hmmmm." His way of saying, "how lovely Scott, but it is too beautiful to drive through." They agreed and the butterflies were happy about that too.

Chapter 19

Wooden Shoes

Having finished a successful cones practice, they headed back to the barn to strategize and talk about what needed to be ready for the show. Scott visualizes movements and gives absolute focus to every aspect of a dressage test or an obstacle on the course, so his head was full of thoughts.

The barn was the medicine he needed, so he cleaned Shadow's stall and fed him just in time for the 5 p.m. hummmm...hmmmmm...hmmmmm. Then he headed out to Angelholm. An idyllic coastal town full of beauty and history. Angelholm was not far and he was looking forward to discovering a restaurant to try while roaming the beautiful cobble stone streets. He explored the village intertwined with beautiful architecture, unique little pottery shops and artisans on the sidewalks. A lovely place to see and share, but for now, only with pictures.

The colorful awning of a quiet little restaurant caught his eye and the aroma of searing meat caught his nose and lead him through the front door. He did not even have to look at a menu as he was escorted to a table passing a heavenly dish still steaming as a patron started to cut their first piece. 'Wiener Schnitzel' said the waiter as Scott just pointed and nodded. The dish was all that it boasted from the presentation to the fork test. That is when he can cut it with just a fork, no knife needed. The veal was moist and flavorful and he enjoyed every bite and a great Swedish beer to wash it down...or maybe two.

On his walk back through the charming town, Scott noticed a pair of wooden shoes in a store window. It reminded him of Gerard's gift of mini wooden shoes that were waiting for him at home. There were two pairs from his years working as a clinician at Gerard Paagman's 'Can Drive' driving camps in the British Columbia Rockies.

At these driving camps, people from all different driving backgrounds and experience levels come and spend a week working with several trainers. Participants try to learn everything they can about all aspects of driving in a stunning location. They enjoy family style dinners and bunk in the great rustic lodging.

Scott had enjoyed his time as a trainer at Can Drive, his grin wide when he thought of his two sets of wooden shoes that were miniatures of the ones Gerard wears every time he sees him. Just thinking of those orange pants and yellow shoes always brings a smile. They are treasured souvenirs of his time there and are signed by many of the other trainers and students at the camps. Too late to get any more as the store was closed, but a nice memory to think about as he went back to his home away from home in the barn next to the 'cute as punch' ponies.

Chapter 20

Nice Pears

Scott headed back to Shadow for his evening walk. The two of them off for an hour walking and talking as they have always done when competing away from home. It is a special time for them to share and one enjoys it as much as the other. Perhaps they talk about living in Sharon and all the training and conditioning that got them here or maybe about the time they were in 'Santa and Rudolf.' Maybe they strategize for the competition next week. Or maybe they just walk together in silence and enjoy each other's company and the comfortable and trusting relationship they have earned over their nearly 10-year partnership.

At the end of the walk a rub on the head and some hay and lights out. Well almost, Scott had a special treat for his buddy. Shadow's favorite things are apples and pears, especially pears. Back in Sharon, Scott had a friend with a large supermarket who would sell him boxes of apples, pears and carrots for the animals. So, when Scott saw the big, ripe pears in the market in Angelholm, he had to get some for Shadow.

When they were back at the stables, he gave him one. Instantly Shadow turned into that messy little boy, pear juice and pulp all over his lips, nose and cheeks. This big, handsome steed was finally content in this strange environment. He looked like 'Messy Marvin' and smelled of pears.

Little did the duo realize what a chuckle they would share the next morning when Jan murmured something about how good the pears were that he found on the camp table. Shadow did not mind sharing!

Chapter 21

British Are Coming

The British Team arrived at the Asplund farm. The contingent was large, four lorries and assorted support vehicles. Three Team drivers and one alternate. Along with their navigators, the head count was around twenty-five...another British Invasion!

The British Team was more than gracious, inviting Scott to their meeting that afternoon and introducing him to everyone in their camp. Once the informalities were over the kidding and wise cracks started, laugher echoed into the evening.

For the first time while living in the barn, there was a knock on his camper door late that night. At first, he thought the 'cute as punch' ponies had learned to knock, but there was a voice.... not the ponies! One of the Brits were looking for the switch to turn off some lights. It was good to have more driving people around the farm.

Before heading to the show grounds, Elsa had planned a great send-off dinner for the United

States and British Teams. An evening everyone was looking forward to. Scott made a visit to the bakery in Angelholm to order pies for the dinner. He got there just to find they had closed for the evening so he could not put his order in. He could see mouthwatering pastries and sweets through the front window, he would definitely be back!

Training camp at the Asplund Stables was nearly over and the next thing on the agenda was packing for the move to the competition grounds. Scott left very early for the Schiphol Airport to get Sue Mallery and Catherine (Cat) Nahmen. Sue was to be his navigator. A competent rider and driver in her own right, and Scott was fortunate to have her on Team Shadow. Cat was a very good horsewoman and had a military background, which Scott always appreciated. She had volunteered to help on the grounds and as most people with military service in their toolbox, she never stopped moving until the job was accomplished. They would be welcome additions indeed!

He hoped to spend a few hours at the Louwman Museum, outside The Hague before their flights arrived in Amsterdam. A lover of fast cars and collectable beauties, he was excited to get the chance to see the amazing collection at Louwman. The most impressive collection he could imagine, in fact considered one of the best in the world. Started and still owned by one family whose grandfather had brought the first Dodge dealership to The Netherlands long ago. Apparently, it paid off. An authentic village set up within the grand museum serving as a dining and resting area for guests. Dozens of shops all fully furnished with early 1900's décor. None of them open for business, but with many windows you could gaze through and travel back in time. A haberdashery, dress shop, barbershop, hotel, candy store, hardware store and even a harness repair shop. Scott's favorite site was the one bay garage servicing an early Dodge. So realistic, with a full array of tools hanging on the wall above the work bench and even a greasy rag left on the fender next to the open hood. It was obvious that the mechanic had just stepped away from his work and would likely return at any moment.

There were not just automobiles, but also carriages, motorcycles, bikes as well as an art gallery. There were rooms for fine china with automobiles on them and vintage airplanes hanging from the ceilings. Even a blimp on display. Last year we visited the Don Garlits Museum in Florida, which was very nice, but Louwman was over the top.

Jan and Elsa had arranged a tour for both Teams at the Royal Stables in Stockholm the day before.

The stables housed the Sweden Royal family's horses and carriages. A fascinating facility and a captivating guide walked them through this magical land. It takes you back in time, to another world of Kings and Queens, processions of horses, carriages and uniforms. They were treated to see areas that the general visitor is not allowed, including a small fleet of the Royalties luxury cars. The guide also enjoyed cars and was the one that told Scott about the Louwman Museum. Just a bonus of the trip and pictures to share at show and tell when he is home again.

Then off to Schiphol Airport in Amsterdam to welcome Cat and Sue to this great adventure. A tour of the training camp and a chance to walk and feed Shadow. Then off to dinner in the little enchanted town of Angelholm that was becoming a nightly ritual. It was comforting to have dinner companions this time.

The next morning Scott went back to the bakery to order the pies for the dinner. Of course, it was too late to place an order. Not to be deterred, and looking at the display case they had just filled with fresh pastries from strawberry pies to cream puffs to eclairs, he said "Can I have them all?" The woman behind the counter smiled in disbelief, but soon realized he was serious. They agreed to sell him the whole case full and would have them all boxed and ready for him later that day. He hoped everyone had a sweet tooth or two.

As he walked out of the bakery with its intoxicating smell of pastries and fresh bread, he nearly bumped into a kindly butcher standing in front of his shop. He was transported back to another time. Seeing his father standing out in front of Monroe's General Store, smiling and thanking a customer for coming in. Here in Angelholm, was the smiling Swedish man with the same white butcher's apron tied in the front and stains of his latest cuts. The butcher nodded a greeting and then walked back into his shop and behind his counter. There it was, exactly like the butcher block his father used for so many years. Worn down on one side with a deep groove where he used it the most.

Scott's father's butcher block was one of his prized possessions and this scene brought back wonderful memories of his dad. This one-hundred-year-old butcher block is always one of the first things you see when you enter Scott's home. This beefy 3' by 3' maple butcher block table is about 18 inches thick and has four round heavy legs. Two people cannot carry it, you need to slide it across the floor. A small reminder of a man he respected as a child and would idolize as he grew into a man.

As he stood there looking at the charming man, he thought of the framed picture of Mr. Monroe smiling in front of the store that hangs in the kitchen of our home in Portland, Maine. A daily reminder of how a family gathering at home to cook meals and eat together is as important today as it had been in his youth. He traveled back to the stables with his head full of memories of his childhood in Cornwall Bridge.

Once the horses were fed, harness cleaned and stored and aisles swept, it was party time. The two nations invaded Jan & Elsa's front lawn with tables and chairs, while the entire Asplund family were preparing a feast in the kitchen. So good to see their four children helping in every phase of preparation and enjoying it! There really are great kids out there, and Scott was glad to witness these four good citizens in the making.

Since the two countries colors are so similar it was hard to tell who-was-who, in the blur of red, white and blue. Each Team member proudly wearing their Country's colors on shirts, hats, jackets and scarves. Beer and wine were chilled, but the Brits brought their secret weapon by the pitcher, Pimm's. Goes down like lemonade but kicks like a mule. Needless to say, the Pimm's was the biggest hit at the party.

The food was delicious and plentiful. Scott snuck in the kitchen before dinner to see a huge pot of meat and vegetables that would become an amazing stew. The colorful assortment of pastries were a luscious addition and Scott personally offered each of the Brits seconds and thirds. The more they eat, the heavier they are, the slower they will go! All is fair in love and war or driving. Soaking up every moment is part of the adventure. Scott was relieved, to see that not one of pastries went to waste.

When the party was over dozens of group photos had been taken and new friendships had been made. Once on the competition grounds, the two Teams continued to help each other out. From towing a dead British ATV back to base camp with Scott's rental car to the Americans getting their carriages power-washed by the British Team after a muddy training lesson and dressage pending the next day. The two countries colors blended many times and, in many ways, the power of Pimm's and pastries.

By the time the show was over, the comrades were swapping Team clothing. They were inviting each other to visit one another's countries for driving trips or just for holiday. New friends made and new memories to cherish, all because of their incredible bond. They raised their glasses to many things that week but never forgotten was the 'real reason' they were all there. The horse.

Chapter 22

Astorp

The morning found Cat, Sue and Scott packing all the harness and equipment needed for the showgrounds into the Asplund's lorry and trailer. Thanks to the kind help of Elsa and Jan they headed off to the World's with Shadow and all they needed for the next week.

Arriving at Astorp's Equestrian Center was an event of its own. This amazing property was within the city limits, which was unusual. The grounds measured over one hundred acres and were breathtaking. The open fields were lined with gorgeous mature European Beech trees. There were ornate gates and huge open expanses bordered by wooded areas. When time permitted, Scott would venture beyond the camp site and would admire beautiful gardens and ancient buildings in good repair and still in use. Truly a feeling of going back in time, while living amid a city.

The day was busy with setting up camp, which consisted of the Asplund's amazing competition trailer. Team Shadow were the ones that felt like royalty now. Once the trailer was detached from the 'lorry' or horse van, this large box trailer converted into very comfortable living and working quarters. Both sides lifted like giant wings to make a large awning on each side. These wings were supported by three posts on either side that suspended it twelve feet in the air. Canvas sides with clear plastic panels were attached to make walls and an equally large covering formed the front door. This was a wonderful thing, as it was the worst summer weather in decades. There was even matting to form a floor covering the ground to keep their feet dry. This proved to be a real treat over the coming days, as the rain continued.

One wing was camp headquarters with a table, benches and chairs and even a fridge, all the comforts of home supplied by Jan and Elsa. The other wing held the carriages and ample space to groom, braid and harness Shadow out of the elements. It rained every day they were in Astorp, making this amazing 'camp' indispensable.

The center section, which was the trailer bed, was used for all the boxes of supplies, harness and all the equipment needed daily. The entire roofline was an open design so you could talk to and hear the entire team no matter where in the 'camp' they were. It was so nice to have a place to get out of the weather to talk and strategize and all the while have Shadow close by.

The lorry was parked kitty corner to the trailer and made a makeshift court yard for cars and outside work. The inside of the van had very nice living quarters and made a great place for drying off from the rain and changing of outfits for the different stages of the event.

The majority of the competitors' encampments were efficient enough, but meager compared to the Asplund caravan. Scott heard another competitor saying that "it was easy to find the American Team, they were down at the end living in luxury." The Americans did not mind a bit! Scott felt bad for the Team from Ireland with little pup tents all around their horse trailer. It rained every day and you know how fun that is in a pup tent. It is ok when you are a kid, but gets old fast when you are past those years and perhaps a little arthritis has set in.

Now the Germans were a different story. They had a long banquet tent about forty feet long. Every night there would be a big dinner and party until early morning. Eruptions of laughter coming from the tent would wake other campers and then subside to lull them back to sleep. Then another joke would be told a short time after and another eruption of laughter would roust those trying to sleep.

Scott took Shadow for a forty-five-minute hand walk to stretch his legs from the trip to Astorp. Scott was thinking how glad he was he had a quiet hotel a half hour from the grounds after hearing how loud the Germans were!

Chapter 23

Game Plan

All this time spent training and practicing was down to a few days and Scott knew how fast this time would fly. He went to the dressage ring and was glad to find it was quiet, but wet. This would allow time to walk the dressage test while not surrounded by the other competitors. It was good to have the arena to himself to walk and think about where transitions of movements should take place. 'Walking' the dressage arena means just that, walking the exact path you will be taking with your horse. A dressage is a choreographed pattern that everyone must complete in an arena in front of Judges.

There were eighteen movements in the dressage test Scott and Shadow would perform. The word 'Dressage' means training in French. The purpose of dressage is to show that a horse is capable of moving at different gaits, at different speeds, at specific moments. Much like the routine figure skaters must perform on an ice rink. The winner, just as in figure skating is the one who gets the best scores from the judges. However, unlike figure skating, driven dressage involves two individuals. The driver must ask for the required movement at the exact letter in the arena and end it at another. Asking is all done through the hands, light requests from the fingers. The horse should look like he is doing the pattern from memory, the driver just along for the ride.

The gaits required call for the horse to use his body in ways to show how talented and gifted he is. Movements such as collection, extensions, stretching, roundness, immobility, lengthening and suppleness are all scored. While the horse performs these movements, he must constantly show a level of relaxation, willingness and understanding of his job. Ironically, a horse does all these movements when it is in a field by itself at different times for different reasons. The difficulty for the driver is to get the horse to perform these 'natural' movements when and for how long the test dictates. This is the challenge of dressage. Riders do the same under saddle, but they have the benefit of using their legs and seat. Drivers only have their hands and a whip to substitute for the aid of the leg. The whip is only used to help the horse, not to punish them, ever.

Scott would spend as much time as possible here, taking notice of landmarks easily seen in or near the course. This would help him remember the exact point of when to ask Shadow for a transition. He would become familiar with the footing and any areas he should be concerned about.

When Scott was back at base camp, he posted the next day's activities on the white board he had stowed in his luggage. This would offer the 'order of go' for the next few days. The second day would consist of practicing the dressage movements with Shadow. The white board had the times everyone had to be on deck and what their assignments were. This was not a drill. Tomorrow was the real deal and Scott wanted everyone rested and ready.

The second day at Astorp's Equestrian Park was again rainy, but everyone was on time and ready for work. Scott had a time slot for the practice arena. In the meantime, he would think about the movements of the dressage test and how he and Shadow would 'make it look easy.' Imagining the movements in his mind and feeling it in his hands which would control Shadow's feet. Scott's saying of 'your hands become his feet' always did the trick.

Scott warmed up in the open field for about forty minutes and then they were on deck to use the practice arena. It was great to have a place set up with letters to practice movements and transitions. Getting a feel of where the quarter lines were and practicing keeping Shadow's impulsion forward but relaxed. He made full use of the thirty minutes he was allotted. Each country received equal time in the practice arena. He left the arena feeling satisfied and headed back to base camp.

Once back at camp, the process of unhitching would commence. Sue would head Shadow by standing in front of him. Meanwhile the over girth, hold back straps and traces were unbuckled. This released Shadow from the shafts of the carriage. Scott led Shadow into his wing of base-camp and Shadow was 'undressed.' This meant that the harness and bridle were removed. A long-standing tradition of removing the sweat marks left by the bridle would begin.

Most horses, having their bridle removed, will rub against you, not unlike a person rubbing their feet after the socks come off. When a horse tries to rub his head on something or someone, it is considered bad manners at the least and dangerous at best. With towel in hand the fun would start!

What Scott started with Shadow long ago, was to have a bath towel at the ready and once the bridle came off, he would rub Shadow's face as hard as he could. Leaning his whole weight into the horse's head and Shadow leaning back the same way as it felt so good. A minute of hard rubbing on his muzzle, cheeks and behind his ears and the horse would shake his head as if to say 'thanks that is enough.' Shadow would get a soft eye and hang his head signifying that it sure felt great, and no additional rubbing would be necessary, 'thank you.'

This routine continues to this day with the same anticipation and results. The headshake and soft eyes still make Scott smile. A friend taking care of a friend. Never a word spoken verbally, but volumes said through the heart.

Chapter 24

Communicator

Next is to remove the studs from Shadow's shoes. Studs are as different and varied as the shoes a person would buy for different sports. The size and shape of a stud or cleat is determined by the footing and job at hand. Not unlike an athlete running or playing soccer. The horse's iron shoes are predrilled to accommodate this threaded stud that is very similar to a screw. They can be put in and taken out at any time. This helps prevent slipping and sliding and avoiding what is called 'losing confidence' for the horse. It is like the studded snow tires you may have on your car. This is one more method of helping keep your horse balanced, because balance is safe when you think like a horse.

Once undressed, Shadow is bathed head to tail. Then all the water is scraped off and a warm wicking sheet put on his back covered by a thin rain sheet. A walk to shake out the practice session and to attempt to dry him off as much as possible in the intermittent rain. Then he was ready for his night blanket and a stall deep in soft shavings with plenty of hay and water. He would surely roll as soon as he got on those clean shavings, but the blanket would keep most of him covered, clean and warm in all the dampness. He had to look his best in the morning for horse inspection, what Scott calls the first phase of any competition.

Every inch of the carriage will be polished in preparation of the dressage test the following afternoon. The harness would be clean and polished to make sure it was ship shape for a proper presentation. Once all this was done the Team would gather at the base camp table and go over the next day's white board assignments and times. Then off for the evening to dine and rest. Mentally preparing for the pressure that would start when morning came.

Scott going over the dressage movements in his head over, and over again as he walked Shadow. Then got his grain and gave him some pointers for the following day. If anyone could 'communicate' with Shadow, it was Scott. Scott knew what Shadow was thinking by the look in his eyes, the movement of his ears and the placement of his feet. Shadow spoke volumes.

One of those luscious pears for Shadow to mess up that immaculately groomed face and he was left to relax and finish his treat.

Chapter 25

Peanut Butter & Jack

The Opening Ceremony was a grand event. Each nation's competitors entered the arena on foot with their entire Team following them. With flags carried high and everyone in full colors of their respective country the Teams entered and formed a large semi-circle around one side of the arena. Little did Scott know that by carrying the American Flag he was starting a tradition he would continue at each of the following World's he was invited to, as a driver or navigator. An honor and a privilege.

A sight to behold and be remembered for years to come, all the colors presented together in unity. The entertainment started with a loud "Let the games begin." Begin they did! Twelve young girls entered riding Shetland ponies and driving a tandem pony in front of each of them with only long reins. They trotted into the arena for a choreographed show, a true 'Kur,' which is a dressage pattern set to music.

The routine was long and complicated, but each rider/driver was as serious and intent on doing their job as were the competitors they were entertaining. But whenever young riders and mischievous ponies are together, additional unplanned amusement is never far behind. As the ponies were changing flanks and crossing within feet of head to tail movements, a few would think it was time to take a snack of the lush grass they were trampling. Soon to get a slap on the butt by the rider behind them to get the dance moving again. The crowd erupted in laughter and applauded the quick fix to let the show go on.

Then the adult riders came out on their beautiful steeds and performed a breathtaking exhibition of dressage movements. For the 'grand finale' all riders entered the ring again. Young and small, mature and large for one last lap around to welcome all the International Competitors and to wish them success.

As the riders departed the arena, each countries' flag was raised on flag poles that surrounded tomorrow's dressage ring. A fitting and moving end to a wonderful opening ceremony. Now onto Nation's Night, let the food begin.

A great night of national pride and community. The Team had great surprises for their guests to try a bit of America. PB & J and Jack Daniels! Many of the international competitors and grooms at the competition had never had peanut butter and jelly, let alone the chance to try a sandwich. After a few samples were handed out to disbelievers, they couldn't make them fast enough. Scott cutting the homemade bread he had found at the bakery in Angelholm...there was no 'Wonder Bread' here!

Sue spreading peanut butter as fast as she could and then Catherine heaping the homemade jam from Momma Lisa's kitchen on the other side of the sandwich. Immediately the gourmet creation was seized. And of course, what better to wash down a PB & J? Jack Daniels of course! Part of the problem with that overweight checked bag, was two carefully packed half gallons of JD.

Dozens of plastic shot glasses in rows, filled to the brim. Lined up perfectly like Marines during a drill. By the end of the evening, it looked like a mini hurricane had hit the American's table. Empty jars, bottles and jam stains everywhere. One thing for sure, all departing friends were smiling!

The entire group was satisfied and happy the United States had pulled off the best Nation's Night treats ever. Mission accomplished.

Cherry Park, Avon, Connecticut. Spencer Sr. in an open wheeled race car on right side of picture . (c. 1939)

Below, Spencer Sr. riding 'Thunder' in Cornwall Bridge, Connecticut (c. 1942)

Spencer Sr. on the porch of his store, arranging produce. (c. 1960)

The Monroe family with Norwegian foreign exchange student Uren Oddnut (far left), wearing the sweaters her mother knitted for the family. Scott seated bottom right. (c. 1957)

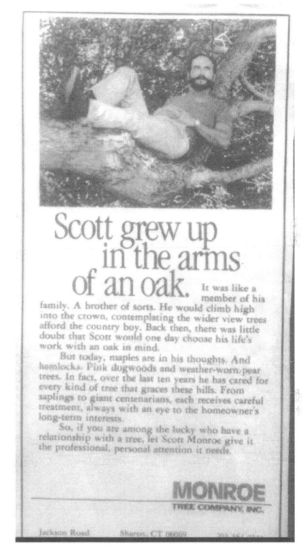
One of many ads run in the local paper to promote Monroe Tree Company as well as Scott's love of trees!

Docile Dawn (c. 1992) Photo by Bonnie Kreitler

*First western riding show with Shadow and for Scott, at
White Tail Farm, Sharon Connecticut. (c. 1998)*

Awaiting the vet check at Gladstone Equestrian
Association CDE. Shadow showing his silly side.
(c. 1998 Photo by Robin Neinstadt)

One of many conversations with Shadow. (c. 2000)

Below, Scott's faithful Labrador, Lucky, along for the drive.

Shadow at Peter Campbell's Natural Horsemanship Clinic in Massachusetts. (c. 2003)   Below, early competition, Shadow's favorite gait- speed. (c. 2000)

Santa and 'Rudolf'
getting ready for their
surprise entrance.
(c. 2004)

Below, driving the
sleigh past his home
in Sharon, Ct.

The herd arrives at Monroe's stable. (c. 2006)

Awaiting the vet check at Garden State Horse Park CDE, in New Jersey. They would go on to win their second consecutive National Championship at this event. (c. 2006)

The Monroe Herd, containing fiberglass cows, miniature donkey Brea, Shadow, Teton & Special.

TPR
Know your horse's normal

Temperature

Adult 99-101 F

Foal 99.5 - 102.1 F

Pulse

Adult 28-44 bpm

(Beats per minute)

Foal 80-100 bpm

Respiration

Adult 10-24

Breaths per minute

Foal 20-40

Breaths per minute

Pratoni Del Vivaro, Italy during World Single Championship. Shadow completes another great cones course.

(c. 2006) Below, all four feet off the ground during Marathon at Gladstone with Sue Mallery. (c. 2007)

Fortune cookies, a little stale after thirteen years!

He who follows his shadow will win in Italy.

'Straw Horse' bringing people together at the Monroe Barn Dance.

Sharon equestrian driven to succeed

JOE
PALLADINO

SHARON

Y ou might say Scott Monroe is driven. At age 40, he took his first lesson driving a carriage. His instructor asked him, "What is your goal?" Monroe replied, "To be a member of the United States equestrian team."

The instructor laughed. Monroe didn't.

Now 54, Monroe is a two-time national driving champion. He drives for his country in the world championships in Italy this month. It is his second time representing America.

And what, might you wonder, is carriage driving? It is a three-phased competition in which a driver, a horse, and carriage compete in dressage, a marathon, and a skill riding competition called cones. It's a little bit about speed, a little more about courage and control, and a lot about trust.

Like any sport that doesn't involve a ball, it is wildly popular in Europe and completely unknown in the New World. All you need to know is that the national champion lives up the road, on a small farm nestled in the deep and quiet of a Sharon forest.

See **DRIVEN**, Page 5

STEVEN VALENTI REPUBLICAN-AMERICAN
Scott Monroe and his horse, Shadow, at home in Sharon.

Interview by sports writer, Joe Palladino, Republican American Newspaper,
Waterbury Connecticut. (c. 2006)

DRIVEN: Monroe ready to take on world

Continued from 1C

EVERYTHING YOU WANT TO KNOW ABOUT CARRIAGE DRIVING

Continued interview with Joe Palladino, Republican American Newspaper.

(c. 2006)

Making a splash at Sunshine State in 2010.

Featured on the front cover of Chronicle of the Horse.

158

The Flying Horse!

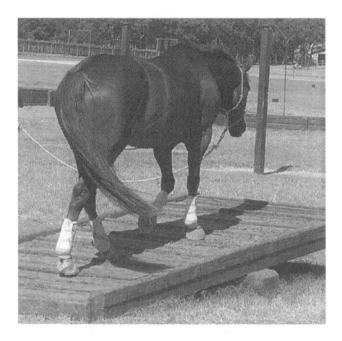

Horse teeter-totter.

Below, practice cones course.

Early ground driving days using a tire as a source of resistance and noise. (c. 1997)

Below, Longlining is a way to perfect the horse's frame and footfall and soft giving hands. (c. 2008)

Scott offers lessons to all ages and abilities. Here giving lessons to my daughter Kate (above) and Jackiellen (Below). (c. 2006)

Another proud moment with Shadow, wearing his very own customized T-(neck)-shirt. (c. 2006)

Visiting with good friend, Gerard Paagman in California.

(c. 2015)

Wooden shoes waiting at home.

Shadow and his stall mate, in the middle white box on the trailer headed to the plane.

Power rollers moving Shadow's box into the plane. Most passengers unaware that horses were aboard.

Giant 'cookie sheets' of the
Team carriages and tack packed
for Europe. (above)

Shadow with his fleece padded
halter getting ready to fly, with
wings this time. (right)

Scott's driving apron and groom
pass for the flight. (below)

Base camp by day, fine dining and beverages by night.

Two of the four
'Cute as Punch' ponies .

Right, Scott giving a
Navigator training clinic
at Gladstone

As a Path Level 2 Driving Instructor, Scott is working with highly decorated Marine Corps Veteran Matt Day at Carlisle Academy. Below, Matt & Scott starting 'Liberty Work' in the round pen. Photos by Jere Gray (c. 2018)

Shadow and Scott blasting through a water obstacle at the Laurels. (c.2006)

Grace wondering if it is 5pm and time for her dinner.

No 'Hmmmm....hmmmmm... hmmmmm...., but a bouf... bouf....bouf.

(c. 2017)

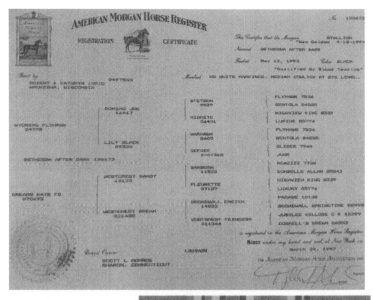

Shadow's lineage (above), Shadow's three National Singles Championship Gold Medals & one special horseshoe. (right)

A small collections of Shadow's awards.

Scott 'following his brother's lead' and enlisting in the Marine Corps.

(c. 1970)

Presently, Jr. Vice Commandant of the Southern Maine Marine Corps Detachment #1824 as well a member of the Honor & Color Guard Teams. Once a Marine, always a Marine.

Chapter 26

Cheshire Cat

Morning finds everyone at base camp preparing for Dressage. Everything from grooming and harnessing to dressing for the presentation. Catherine had been a total surprise volunteer for the Team and a great help. From bringing fresh fruit for camp every morning to helping groom and harness Shadow, to spreading jam. Volunteers make this sport and we are always thankful for them!

Dressage times had been posted as well as practice times in assigned arenas. Scott and Shadow headed off to the warm up field, where he had twenty-five minutes, then twenty minutes in the dressage practice area. This is when Sue would take her position in the groom's set behind Scott. At the Advanced and FEI Level, a groom is required to be on the carriage whenever in an area with officials in attendance. Ten minutes before his go time they would be called across the road to be on deck for the official arena. As the prior competitor exited the arena and the bell was rung, he would have ninety seconds, just enough time for a couple figure eights and then entered the arena on the center line. Show time. Shadow had to halt in the center of the arena at the 'X' and be immobile while Scott gave his first salute to the head judge at the front of the arena. It felt like slow motion and Scott could not even see Shadow breathing, he knew how important this was for his human. The transitions up and down through all movements were smooth and precise. Time can stand still in the dressage ring, but before they knew it, they were coming up the center line for their final salute. The head judge saluted and away they drove hearing the crowd loudly applauding. The smile on Scott's face was no less than that of the 'Cheshire cat.' The greatest compliment to a driver is that they make the dressage test look easy, and Shadow and Scott did just that!

Chapter 27

Countdown

Dressage behind them, but their day was not over. Thanks to the wind and a partially dry day, the grounds had dried enough to allow Scott and Sue to easily bike the course and walk each hazard. Drivers must learn to memorize the eight obstacles, each having six gates. They walked the course until they were confident in their patterns or it was just too dark to continue.

Catherine was getting the marathon carriage ready and setting out hoof boots, helmets, safety vests, timecards, carriage number and whip for the start time the following morning. When they returned from the course, it was time for Shadow's evening walk. The walk was a good time to give Shadow a pep-talk for the following day, Marathon day. When these good friends returned to the barn, Scott gave Shadow some hay, topped off the water and put his night blanket on him, tucking him in for the night.

There are three parts to a Combined Driving Event. We talked about Cones in Chapter 18 and Dressage in Chapter 23, but the most exciting phase is the Marathon. The marathon is 'to test the fitness, stamina and training of the Horses, and the driving skill, judgement of pace and general horsemanship of the Athlete.'

Marathons at this level are three-sections long. Section A is more of a cross-country course with a distance to be traveled in a certain amount of time. You can choose your pace, if you meet the time requirements. After Section A, there is a Walk (transfer) section. This needs to be done at the walk, but still within the window of time. There is a veterinarian after the walk section, before you can start Section B, to monitor the health and wellbeing of each horse.

Section B can have as many as eight obstacles, lettered A-F for each driver to maneuver through. They can be made of anything from wood to rocks to water or even within a natural stand of trees. They are marked with lettered gates to travel through in order, very similar to the numbers in a Cones course. You cannot go through them out of order or penalties will be invoked. Obstacles must be driven at great speed and Shadow loves them!

He revs up like a race car and barrels into each maze of the course with the spirit of the wind.

Sue as the navigator, would be riding on the back during the marathon for counterweight and navigation, and had to memorize the course as well. Navigators, who stand on the back of the carriage are an essential part of the team during the marathon phase. They help keep the carriage wheels down. They also use their weight and foot placement on the carriage to help on fast corners and can even help shimmy the carriage over in a tight turn.

Since each kilometer must be covered in a predetermined amount of time, Sue keeps track of the time and the K's on the marathon as well as any possible hold times. This keeps them on schedule throughout the course. The 'gator' is also an extra hand when needed and an extra guide through the course to help the driver stay on the right path. An invaluable member of any team.

Shadow, ever responsive to the slightest touch of Scott's hands through the reins. The years of Scott's fine tuning this one-horse power engine will enable him to take the throttle and roar through the marathon. Fourteen days away from home, it will all be worth it.

Marathon day comes early, and Scott and Sue are there before the rest of the team to see how dry the course is and to finish the last-minute preparations. The entire team was there at 0700 so Scott can go over everyone's job and timing for the morning. Then he heads out to walk the marathon course one last time before the first competitor is on the course. This gave him an opportunity to finalize his attack plan. Attacking a course is exactly what you need to do, as it is the course designer's intent to make the course extremely challenging. They want to test the driver, to see how they handle their horses around the hairpin turns, uneven terrain, change of footing and unforgiving trails.

Once the first competitors were on course Scott got a chance to watch some of them go. He wanted to see where footing was a problem and where the grade could be an issue. His first concern was safety, after that it was doing everything in his power to take home a gold medal.

The team was getting Shadow prepared for a 1300 go time. Scott did not want to allow for too much warm-up time so Shadow could conserve his energy. He had watched the countdowns that morning at the beginning of Section A, and they were called out in Swedish. He tried to remember the order of words so he could start at the right signal. To his surprise and delight, the countdown was called in English for them and they were ready, 10, 9, 8 and they were off!

Section A was through overgrown fields that had patches of mowed grass and sections that were just trampled down. The footing was soft and tough going, the constant rain certainly did not help.

They were soaked, but for a brief time the rain subsided for just a few minutes. There must have been some timing issues or problems with the horses ahead of them on the course because they were held before the walk section. It was crowded and the horses did not want to stand still. Mass confusion seemed to be looming in the heavy damp air. Scott was a little edgy about the situation, when suddenly, he glanced down at his left hand. There perched on his wrist looking him square in the eye, was a beautiful butterfly. Just like the ones he and Shadow had seen a few days before dancing over the 'field of flowers.' This elegant and graceful creature looked at him and slowly lowered and raised his wings as if directing Scott to breathe to the rhythm of each movement. Scott smiled and a sense of relief came over him and he softly whispered 'thank you' to his new winged friend. One more gentle flutter, a final glance and off the butterfly flew. Perhaps a gesture of appreciation of the pair not racing through the Swedish 'field of flowers.' The reason for the visit did not matter as it was just the medicine Scott needed. A sign to him that they would have a successful and safe competition that day.

When they finally reached the hold area before Section B, Cat was waiting with water buckets for Shadow to drink and to cool him off. The vet inspection was uneventful. When released from the Vet box, they walked to the start of Section B and waited for their 'English' countdown.

Chapter 28

Ol' Cow Pony

When the countdown starts, so does the fuel injection in this eleven-year-old Morgan. Shadow knew his job and he loved it. Turning the corner, he saw it. Even though it was one kilometer before they entered the first obstacle, Shadow became even stronger. Much like the Grinch whose heart grew three times in size. He had not gained the reputation of the 'Marathon Horse' for nothing.

The first obstacle is an opportunity to work on your timing, how the conditions will affect your horse and shake off any last-minute jitters. The rain was coming down, but regardless, hundreds of people were gathering around each obstacle to support the competitors. The sport of Combined Driving is very popular in Europe. Besides having a longer history with horses in general, driving is as much a part of their lives as baseball is to us. When the functionality of driving was left behind with the advent of automobiles in our country, the Europeans not only kept the tradition, but perfected it into today's Combined Driving Events. No wonder they are the best of the best. The crowds are not only a great motivator, but a confidence builder for the drivers.

There would be dead silence when the nose of a horse breaks the entrance gate, starting the time clock. One must go through all the gates A thru F in order as quickly as possible in the least amount of time. Like a seasoned professional, Shadow would fly through the obstacle like greased lightning. The clock stops as the horse's nose comes across the exit gate. At this level of competition, electronic timers are used to eliminate human error.

The silence of the crowd turns to roars of enthusiasm as Shadow flies through the obstacle. Once through the end gate, he would easily drop into a slow trot and conserve his energy for the next obstacle, like an 'ol cow pony.' He knew how to play this game and he played it well.

Obstacle two appears and like a light switch Shadow turns into a lightning bolt. Scott finesses his way through the obstacle, maneuvering the horse and carriage through very tight turns. Then thundering through the end gate at a runaway gallop stopping the clock.

Then the ol' cow pony appears again, downshifting to a slow trot to save energy until the next pull of the pin ball game is taken. Obstacle three, four, five, six and seven were taken down all in the same manner. Eight was a bit trickier and one deviation of course was made and quickly corrected. This added some time penalty points, but no more than the other competitors already had. No harm done.

One of the big differences between this and the events at home, was the lack of traffic control or crossing guards. This was a park and was open to the public. There were baby strollers, umbrellas, groups of ten to twenty people crossing the roads and trails at a time. Cars and groups of cyclists going through intersections that were part of the course with no mind to the horses speeding through. Here in Europe seeing driving horses everywhere was a common everyday occurrence. At one point they were coming through a gate and a car came within seconds of hitting them. Perhaps a Guardian Angel was 'following Shadow' too. Scott decided he would never complain about traffic on a marathon course in the United States again!

The marathon was free of costly penalties, accidents or eliminations for the whole US Team, this was indeed a good day. They would not be taking home any gold, but mission accomplished. Like many high-level athletic events, to finish is to win. The amount of penalties and infractions one can accumulate during an event is staggering. With all that to contend with, winning or even placing is a great accomplishment. Being in the top three, whether Nationally or Internationally is a thrill and rush to match any sport.

Back at camp the ritual of undressing, bathing and walking Shadow ensued, it would be a busy evening for the team. Scott was thankful Cat and Sue knew the drill well and Shadow trusted them and was relaxed in their company.

Shadow would need three walks that afternoon into the evening, about thirty minutes each. An equal amount of time both walking and resting in his stall would help to flush out the build-up of lactic acid from his system after such a high level of physical work. Not such bad duty for Scott and Shadow who enjoyed their walks together, made even better on this beautiful property in Sweden.

Chapter 29

Cowboy Hats & Used Shirts

The next day was even more interesting. All three of the United States Team members drove the cones course in white cowboy hats, in the pouring rain. Two of the Team drove the course double clear. Scott was the last of the three to drive as he had the best score going into the cones phase.

After seeing both his Teammates drive double clear, he knew the pressure was on. Not unlike any critical challenge, Scott knew that nerves could be detrimental and blocked everything out. Location, sound, standings were gone. Once again it was he and his unwavering partner given a challenge many only dream about. They would be in their own zone, even unaware that Sue was sitting beside him. When he entered the start gate, his heart stopped racing, respiration became normal, there was a job to perform and an adventure to experience. Everything was going perfectly until he approached the seventeenth set of cones. Normally during cones, spectators are very respectful, and a pin could be heard hitting the ground. But as he approached set seventeen, a huge gasp resonated from the crowd. As well as he could block out the world in his mind, this was too much.

His years of experience told him to ignore what he heard, what it could mean? Just drive on, because the words quit and can't are not in a Marine's vocabulary. They cantered through cones 18, 19 and 20 and across the finish line... the crowd roared!

They had gone double clear, no penalties. Coach Singer was waiting at the arena exit gate in anticipation. Scott's first question was, "why did the crowd gasp at cone 17?" His coach gladly answered, "Because they were watching the clock! They wanted to witness the first Team from any country to ever have all their members drive the cones course double clear at a world's championship! Must have been the white cowboy hats!"

Scott finished 12th in the world and was the highest overall scoring American on the Team. What was an extra delight was that Scott was now part of the 'drive off' for cones, a great honor at this level of combined driving.

Out of the nearly eighty competitors at this world level competition, there were only six that drove the cones double clear and three were the Cowboys. These six were to drive it again with a few less cones, try to be double clear and of those who were, the best time would win. This would not change your standings in the competition, but it was a party that few were invited to.

Scott and Shadow drove it double clear, not the time winners, but satisfied to have accomplished this and proud as punch to be representing the United States once again, but this time in a different uniform.

The thrill and emotions were difficult to explain but would be cherished forever. That moment when you let down your guard and hear the crowd can throw your whole game. You need to stay the course and finish as strong as you started. This was a lesson Scott learned many times in the military, in his driving career and in his life. He tries to pass it on to his driving students when they feel they have lost after knocking down a ball in one of his cone courses. He tells them to stay focused because their competitor might knock down two. Or even be unlucky enough to not only knock down a cone but have it become stuck to the bottom of the carriage and drag it out of the arena!

Once the exciting cones run off was over, the Team headed back to camp, their heads spinning from the day and the excitement. Filled with the thrill of all they had seen, disappointed that there would be no medals going home with Shadow, but no one would let this cloud the grandness of the event for an instant.

Elsa and Jan were there to cheer on their new friends and to help break down camp. Scott was busy tearing down and packing up and he glanced around to see Sue and Cat surrounded by the Brits, laughing with their allies, halfway around the world. Happy to share this time with them and sad to be leaving, to have this adventure coming to an end. Scott always says to "Enjoy the Moment," his team was, and this made him smile. The memories and friends they take home in their heart would be worth more than gold, silver or bronze.

Soon the trading began, each Team member with their home country's clothing, hats and pins eager to swap. Prepared for this, Scott had brought extra Team hats and many USA shirts for the Team to use for 'trades' to fill their souvenir chests from this amazing adventure. Part of the reason for the extra luggage fee! It was a great way to share some of your country with all the new friends, and perhaps foes, that you made during the week.

The Team Coach from France wanted a shirt from the driver with the 'Cheval Volant.' Scott did not know what he was asking and looked at him with a puzzled expression. The Italian coach laughed and said "Cavallo Volante," the crowd started to laugh and call out the words in their own languages. 'The Flying Horse.' It seems that Shadow had been given a new nickname. Not just because he flew to Amsterdam, but because many competitors and spectators were sure they saw him fly through the obstacles during the marathon!

When the last deal was made and the last hug given, everyone returned to their respective camps and continued to pack. The Americans joking that if they had more peanut butter and jam to trade who knows what they would be going home with!

Each country's trucks, vans and trailers began to pull away one by one. Each human and horse tired, but happy to have been part of this adventure and glad to have so many new friends around the world, all brought together... by the horse.

Chapter 30

Nice Pair

Jan and Else drove the lorry back to their stables and Scott headed to the Schiphol Airport to drop off Sue and Cat. They would stay at a hotel next to the airport and fly out early in the morning. They had been invaluable on this European adventure and Scott hated to see them go. Their souvenirs stowed safely in their carry-on as they were not letting them out of their sight. As much as Scott wanted to sit with them and talk about the last few days events, he really needed to get back the Asplund Stables and to his 'Cheval Volant.'

So many thoughts filled his head while he drove back. Hearing Shadow's new nickname made him a little embarrassed that he did not understand the incredible compliment. He understood 'cheval,' but was stumped by 'volant.' His French vocabulary not exactly what it should have been for someone who took a class on the language in grammar school. Just a handful of words and phrases he could speak with authority and reverence. Perhaps it would have been larger if he had not been thrown out of his French class!   It would seem, that his matronly teacher did not find it amusing when he brought his 'Hot Rod' magazine to class. Opening the center pinup for all to see and commenting on what a 'nice pair' it pictured...a pair of dual carbs!

After a visit to the school by his parents, that was the end of French class for Scott.   Apparently, his teacher did not share his love for fast cars or a nice pair of carburetors.

Scott's parents, who did not condone his behavior, did share this fascination with cars. Spencer senior raced open wheeled cars on the oval track as a young man in the 1930's, Scott has pictures of those early days. As well as a picture of his dad on a big bay horse, 'Thunder,' which may explain the riding that seems to be in Scott's genes.

His mother Ruth loved the little red 1968 Opel GT she was given by his dad. The car was a gift to show appreciation for all her years of hard work raising five children, Scott being the last. It was her fun car and she loved to take it for long drives or just to see it in the yard. One morning however, while Scott was home on leave, she woke to see her precious toy across the street at the local garage, hanging on the wrecker's hook, not quite as shiny as it had been the day before.   Seems a certain young man may have skid off the road with it coming in late the night before. She would not even speak to him, so he returned to duty before his leave was over without a single word from her. She had forgiven him, but it took a while!

As he drove back to the stable, he could see Ruth standing beside the road with an American flag in her hand, waving as he and Billy drove off. He looked forward to telling her tales about his trip and Shadow's new French name.

Like any other show, he would go over every phase of the event analyzing what he could have done better and where he and Shadow could improve. This Marine wanted to do his best, to do his job and do it right. Twelfth in the world was not only a great achievement, but also a personal challenge to do better next time.

Chapter 31

Rear Guard

Shadow was in his stall munching on his hay at the Asplund Stable when Scott arrived. The hmmmmmm... hmmmmm... hmmmmm of dinnertime was the first sound he heard. Then the 'cute as punch' ponies chiming in. They had already been fed and Scott was not falling for that old trick!

Elsa had taken Shadow for his walk already and Scott could see the fatigue of the last few days in those big, dark soft eyes. Pears were the answer and he just so happened to have stopped at a roadside market on the way back from Schiphol airport. A big juicy one in his feed bucket and a rub on the forehead for 'Cheval Volant.'

Morning came and with it the coos of the mourning doves and the whinnies of horses. Scott was feeling like the rear guard. The rest of Team Shadow were on their long journey home and he and Shadow were bringing up the rear. Not unlike the first few days here, it was just the two of them again. Long walks, long talks, getting ready for their next adventure.

Martin helped Scott pack the carriage, cart, harness and all the tack onto two pallets. Then it would be delivered to the freight forwarder in Amsterdam for shipment back to the East Coast.

When competing in Europe you have two options about equipment and carriages. You can arrange to lease everything or bring your own. Shipping two carriages is costly but the main reason for using your own gear is the consistency of your performance. You know your horse is comfortable in his own harness and carriages. That is impossible to recreate at training camp with new equipment. Your carriages are an extension of you and the harness connects you to your horse. When assembled, your turnout is one entity and to exchange parts of it diminishes the whole.

Another reason is the memories, every time you sit in that carriage, see that harness, leg boots and driving gloves, you think of where they were used. What they accomplished and what they represented. Those memories will never end. For now, all those items were palletized, wrapped and headed back home.

The next day started like all the rest during training camp. Alarm rang at 0545, Shadow's stall cleaned, morning hay given, and water topped off. Several carrots, to accompany the grain. Scott got a kick out of the carrots available in the local market, leafy tops and all. They looked like they had just been pulled out of the garden. Shadow liked them too, greens with his crunchies, a bonus.

Then Scott would head off for his run. The distance became longer and harder each day. Not because he was getting tired but because the turn-around point changed every day. What was around the next corner? Could it be any prettier than this? It was. The fields of onions and beets turned to row after row of glass greenhouses growing tomatoes, cucumbers and peppers. Earthen mounds of soil formed into huge water holding basins. The landscaping was immaculately maintained around each hot house facility. These year-round and climate-controlled greenhouses are probably the future of agriculture. But for now, they share the fields with yesteryears' forms of producing our vegetables. No matter the era of farming, it was all beautiful to look at and the grass always seemed to be greener over the next fence.

Back to the barn and off to Shadow's first walk of the day, one of the last with Scott on Swedish soil.

There was little use for bug spray as there were few insects to bother Shadow. The ones that did attack, Scott called 'horse vampires.' They were as large as the 'horse' or 'moose' flies on the East Coast. Scott would practice his slap timing. Not quite as fast or nimble as the famous karate teacher who could catch a fly with chopsticks, but darn close. Shadow never jumped when Scott would get the flies, he knew what was coming and why. He was always appreciative.

After a long drink in his stall, Shadow offered his "hummmm.... hmmmmm and Scott weakened a bit on his feeding rules and gave him more hay and a pear. A few extra pounds going into the long flight was a good thing. Horses can drop quite a bit of weight during a long journey like this. Too bad it was not that easy for the rest of us to drop a few pounds!

Chapter 32

Souvenirs

Not much left to pack or prep for the 'flying horse.' His special halter and four bell boots are hanging on the stall door for tomorrow. These boots are fleeced lined, so as not to chaff his legs while wearing them. They are to protect him from injuring himself while trying to stabilize during turbulence. The halter is also fleeced lined to protect his face from rubbing, like a fuzzy pair of socks separating your foot from a boot. Even with the fleece, Scott knows Shadow would love a head rub when the halter comes off in quarantine many hours from now. He wished he could be there to give him one, so didn't Shadow.

Now it was Scott's turn to pack. He had hoped to save the $100 overweight luggage fee on the return flight. It should be lighter without the peanut butter, jam, Jack Daniels, the 'trading' USA shirts, hats, 75 small American flags, banners, red, white and blue napkins and plates for Nation's Night.

Without the glass maple leaf shaped bottles of Maine maple syrup for a few special friends, surely it would be under the weight limit. He would soon learn that it wasn't. Must have been the ten-gallon white western hat that the Team Coach gave each of the drivers for cones. Or was it the heavy duty, waterproof Team jacket from the Italian Coach? Maybe the added weight of the mud boots that had been so helpful during this week of rain. Probably what pushed the bag over the proverbial edge were the glasses.

Those beautiful etched glasses, with swirling cut edges at the base for grip that disappeared into thin etched lines as they twisted all the way to the rim. Not just any kind of glasses mind you, but Scott's beer glasses, a box full. His favorite restaurant was in Angelholm. They served a great draft beer in glasses that advertised the brand. He tried to buy some, but they were not for sale. The restaurant was a class act and simple touches like the glasses made it even more enjoyable. Martin the manager, the second kind Martin that Scott had met on his trip, was certainly one of the reasons the restaurant was so successful.

By the end of Scott's stay after many nights at this eatery, Martin presented him with a full set of his favorite glasses, unfortunately minus the beer! The glasses and Italian jacket were not unlike the memories Sue and Cat had packed in their treasures of the trip, to enjoy for years to come.

He packed the rest of his belongings, he would be home soon. Looking forward to raising one of the beautifully made beer glasses for a toast, thinking of all the great memories made in Sweden. A toast, not with Swedish beer, but with Mexican, to happy days with great people and one amazing horse!

Chapter 33

Mondays

Monday at Asplund Stable is 'stall cleaning day,' and when you have over eighty boarded horses and forty of your own, cleaning stalls is no minor operation. Their system does make it as simple and efficient as one could imagine, and it was very impressive to see.

Visualize the wall between each stall being on tracks that could be pulled out into the isle. As each wall is pulled into the aisle to form a new stall the horse is lead through the stall door, turned around and hooked to the other side of the door, new stall! This allowed a tractor to drive from one end of the barn to another. Because they use straw for the horse bedding, the tractor has a combination of a bucket and a grapple that scrapes and grabs all the bedding up and out. It is then dumped into an awaiting trailer at the end of the barn and taken to be used as mulch at a local mushroom farm. Nothing is wasted here, the ultimate recycling.

The stall striping starts at 9 a.m. and finished by 3 p.m. The stalls are swept, another tractor with a trailer carrying a large bale of straw is pulled into the open lane. Stopping at each stall space, a 'flake' of this enormous bale is pulled off and dropped in the stall. Then the stall walls rolled back into place. A simple and ingenious way to clean so many stalls at once. The horses are walked back into their original stall and the crew moves to the next barn.

While all this is going on it makes for an ideal time to take Shadow for another walk. He tolerates the noise and commotion, but why put him through it when the fields bring such tranquility. By late afternoon they were back at the stables and Shadow was thinking about dinner, so was Scott.

The barn is quiet now, not the usual hustle and bustle of training and grooming, as Monday is a day off for all the horses. Riders who boarded their horses there would start arriving later in the evening after their workday was done. For now, they enjoyed the quiet time together.

Shadow was always one of those horses that thinks he must be 'involved' with or at least see what is going on in the aisle, no matter where in the world he is. Scott has spoiled him a bit by leaving his stall door open and a simple lead line hanging across the opening to hold him in. When Shadow was young and challenging, he would go under the lead line. Usually only as far as the 'greener grass' was, hmmmmm, wonder who he got that idea from? In his later years doing the 'limbo' was not an option he wanted to consider anymore. Besides, he had learned that eventually food will be brought to him.

So, the pair, hang out at the stall together, like they so often did. Scott sitting on a bag of shavings he pulled over in front of the stall opening and Shadow resting his chin on Scott's head. The scene is touching and picturesque, until Shadow snorts! Then it can be quite messy, but a small price to pay. One must realize there is a trade-off for everything. This is one Scott would take any day.

These two friends just hang out. Scott going over the paperwork and flight schedule for Amsterdam. Shadow watching him reading his paperwork and wondering how many more minutes until dinner. Would have been a nice memory to share if someone had been there with a camera.

Dinner was served, at least for Shadow. His mixture of grain and supplements topped with a fresh array of carrots and an apple. Scott's dinner would be back at his favorite restaurant in Angelholm, but this time with the Asplund family as his guests. A price could not be put on the little camper in the corner of the barn with Shadow and the 'cute as punch' ponies, so they agreed on dinner. Another fantastic meal. Ordering fish is never a problem when you can see the water. Here the water was everywhere, and the fish was amazing.

When back at the stable, Scott took Shadow on their last Swedish walk as the final light from the sunset was fading. A pear, night hay for Shadow and lights out in the little trailer beside the 'cute as punch' ponies for Scott. The soft munching of the horses sounded like rain on the roof and this was a lullaby that quickly put Scott to sleep.

Chapter 34

Apples

Earlier morning than usual, 0445, as Scott wanted Shadow to get at least an hour of eating his hay while motionless. Something that was going to be in short supply for many hours to come. Scott loaded Shadow into the trailer at 0600 to head to Schiphol Airport for the last time. Martin drove Shadow in the horse trailer, while Scott followed closely behind with the rental car and they arrived at the airport at 0730. The main entrance was under heavy security. Every vehicle stopped and inspected, from mirrors under the cars to opening every door and trunk. But for some reason they had free sailing into the cargo area of this enormous airport. They delivered Shadow to the Animal Hotel for flight preparation. Once the paperwork was all set, Scott walked Shadow into the air box and left to return his car. There is no 'hold time' or quarantine period when leaving Europe for some reason. If the paperwork is in order, the horses are immediately loaded in the air boxes. They would nibble on their hanging hay nets for a few hours until Scott could make his way to the rear of the plane.

Then off to get himself and his luggage checked in for the flight. Of course, his luggage still over the weight limits, but this time only a $75 charge.

The inside of the airport was as impressive as it was crowded. Airport security was intense and downright intimidating. There were armed and vested security personnel everywhere. Bomb sniffing dogs and police walking around with automatic weapons. Lines were long and the waiting was weighting heavy on Scott's mind, he could not miss Shadow's flight.

He waited in line only to find the tickets they had given him when he checked in were for a flight that left fifteen minutes before. He had missed the flight Shadow was on. He called home to say he had missed Shadow's flight and he would be stuck in Amsterdam until he could get another flight back to JFK. He was very upset to think of Shadow not seeing him on the plane. Not seeing that look of relief in those big soft eyes. Not hearing that "hummmmm... hmmmmm... hmmmm" that meant he was hungry and that he was glad to see Scott. Letting Shadow down was not a good feeling, but he could do nothing but wait in line two more hours trying to get home.

When he finally got to the front of the line, they told him he did not miss his flight. Better still was that Shadow was still there, on the plane they were both supposed to be on to begin with. The agent had printed the wrong ticket for him and apologized for the confusion. A sense of relief came over him, but he still did not have a ticket in his hand. It was now 2 p.m., and Scott knew that Shadow was ready for one of their countryside walks. That wasn't happening today. The best he was going to get was a few juicy apples to break up the last of the European hay. That was if he and his carry-on bag made it on the flight.

Thirty more minutes in line and there was news that the flight was boarding humans. He just wanted to get on that plane. Finally, he had a ticket in his hand and off to the plane he rushed. A seat second to the last row by the galley. A quick meeting with the other grooms for the flight and then back to see Shadow. Once the canvas flaps were flipped open and the horses visible, the look of relief was there in Shadow's eyes and the "hummmmm" softer and lower than normal. Perhaps saying "there you are... I was getting worried." Scott stood with Shadow and his roommate and steadied them for take-off. The other grooms did the same in their assigned air boxes. There were fourteen horses on the flight, and most were three to a box, but Shadow had just one stall mate.

Scott had packed as many apples as he could fit in his carry-on bag, perhaps breaking some rules, but he figured if he had gotten through that much security it must have been alright. He gave some to the other grooms to share with the horses they had in tow and offered one to Shadow and his roomie.

Back and forth to see the horses several times and teasing them about "eating like it was free" as his mother would say about him and his sister Sue. Sue, who he deeply missed as he had lost her a few years ago to cancer. She and Scott were very close, and she was so much like their father. Scott smiled as he thought of her and 'free food.' He thought about his father sending cases of oranges to the local elementary school every Christmas for all the children. This tradition started because when his father was a child, his family was so poor, a single orange was the only gift he and his siblings would receive. A small gesture to perhaps remind them of the simple pleasures in life and how they should be appreciated and shared. Sue took this lesson to heart. After her four children graduated from college, she enjoyed spending many years as a teacher's aide. She became a second mother to many students and some never even knew who to thank. She would quietly buy clothes for those that needed them or pay for their school lunches. In a very small way, Scott with his bag of apples was trying to make a stressful trip for the horses a little more enjoyable. So many good memories from his youth, and so many more he was bringing home from Sweden.

Chapter 35

Flying Horse

During the flight, Scott and Shadow were surprised to have the pilot come and visit them in the cargo area. Apparently, pilots and co-pilots take turns checking on the cargo, especially if it is horses they are responsible for. Well of course, you know who the favorite of the horses would be.

Scott made several trips back to check on the 'flying horse' and his roomie. Seems that Shadow was always looking for another treat and ready to drink the water Scott offered him, a very important sign when moving a horse, especially at 36,000 feet. Anyone with horses knows that hay sticks to everything and the smell of horses is unmistakable. Then add the fact that you are in a confined space of an airplane, the secret cargo can be detected. So was the case here, when several 'horsey' passengers wanted to know where Scott was going and why he had hay on his shirt and jeans. They were intrigued by the thought of horses right behind them. Where had they been, where were they going, how many were back there and of course... can we go see

215

them? The flying horse was again bringing complete strangers together, sharing their stories. Scott asked the head groom if he could take the other passengers back to see the horses. They could not go into the cargo bay but could peek through the doorway. Smiles on every face and 'the flying horse' looked towards the door with his ears perked up and that expressive face that warms the soul. He was hoping he would have a new group of fans that could come and pet him and perhaps bring him a snack! Not today, but he certainly made some more humans happy and gave them more stories to tell.

When the nine-hour flight was close to an end, Scott was there with the horses, calming them for landing. A smooth landing and as soon as they had taxied, the big cargo doors opened letting in the New York air. A veterinarian boarded the plane and drew blood from each horse. The blood was sent to Ohio for testing, if nothing negative was found, it would be 48-72 hours before they would be cleared to go home. From here until the horses enter the quarantine area, their 'feet cannot touch the ground." Scott had to say goodbye to Shadow, a head rub and a kiss on his apple covered nose and he had to close the flaps on the air box.

A conveyor elevator was wheeled to the cargo door and the air boxes were slowly rolled off the plane. When they were on the elevator it was lowered close to the tarmac, Scott and the other traveling grooms were not allowed to touch the horses and could just standby watching their horses as they were taken away for quarantine. Then the entire platform was driven over to a high sided walkway that would keep the horses 'off the ground.' Each air box was opened by grooms who worked for the horse haulers. One by one the horses were led out, and onto the walkway. A single glance back from Shadow and he was gone. Through the high sided shoot and into an awaiting horse trailer. When each trailer was full, the side ramp was lifted and closed and a padlock secured the door.

Scott watched as the large horse vans drove out of sight, hung his head and walked back into the main terminal of the airport. A feeling of loss overtook him as he walked away. He worried what was going through Shadow's mind and he hoped that he knew Scott would be there as soon as he could.

Scott got a ride home with one of the other Team members, feeling he had left so much behind. He knew as a Marine, that procedures and rules were in place for a reason and this was just the way it had to be.

One of the first things he did was go to the barn and make sure things were ready for 'the flying horse' to return.

Chapter 36

In My Pocket

It was good to be home, or at least not moving for a while. Like with any separate project or vacation, once it is over, you remember life was still going on while you were gone. Scott's business needed catching up with as well as everyday problems to be addressed. He really did not mind hitting the ground running, he was used to it. What he did mind was not having his horse home with him. Knowing or at least hoping, Shadow's blood work would come back with no problems. One never knows what horses pick up between the traveling, new locations and proximity to so many foreign horses, not unlike people.

Forty-eight hours can seem like forever and Scott answered the phone on the first ring. Shadow had been cleared and he could pick him up. The truck and trailer already hitched, off to Newburg, New York and the holding center.

He drove to the warehouse where his carriages, harness and tack had been stored and was disgusted to find it all covered with a white chalky solution that smelled of disinfectant. The attendants even sprayed his boots with the solution before they let him enter the facility. Another necessary procedure, but none the less annoying.

When everything was loaded and secured on the flatbed truck, another hour wait for Shadow. Finally, a man walked down the path towards him with Shadow on a lead line and a clipboard under his arm. Once Scott could verify that it was in fact his horse and signed the paper, he rubbed that soft nose and wrapped his arms around the neck of his 'Cheval Volant.'

Shadow was happy to enter his own trailer, with hay from home and of course a big fat pear on top. Scott could feel the sense of relief in both he and his horse. Once Shadow was settled in the trailer and had a big drink of water, they headed home.

The word soon spread to his supporters that Shadow had done them proud. Scott's goal was to medal of course, as with every competitor. Or at least be within the top ten in the world, but they were close at 12th. No big parties, no memorable moments, but glad to be back in the groove of normal life.

With the absentee problems solved and lost sleep regained, his thoughts drifted to 2006. The next World's Single Championship would be in Italy. Recording where his performance was weak and what worked, a new training schedule for 2006 was formulated.

Competing one horse is the least expensive way to be part of this equestrian discipline. But it is also the riskiest. Horses, like human athletes, must stay in shape between competitions, but not overdo it either. They call it 'letting your horse down,' meaning backing off on their fitness program to save them. Scott always has says, "There are only so many miles in those legs, choose them wisely."

It was one of Shadow's days off, but not for Scott. A stressful day and Scott wanted to take a long walk and wanted some company. So, he and Shadow headed up the town road that would lead to the 'old farm at the four corners.' He was hoping to get there by sunset, as the terrain dropped off to the west exposing spectacular sunsets for those lucky enough to know the spot. They walked together past the sugar maples, enjoying the night air and the presence of a few mature American Elms still standing. It was a beautiful evening and the sun started to sink in the sky. The two just appreciating each other's company and every once in a while, a low "hmmmmm" from Shadow as if he were commenting about the changing colors in the sky as he munched the tall grass.

As the sun was sinking low, the two headed back down the town road towards home. Glad to be on United States soil and glad that there was no traffic, feeling as if they owned the road. Shadows began to form on the sides of the road, outlining the rows of sugar maples and elms. Between the trees were the long shadows of a man and his horse.

Scott smiled and chuckled to himself, or perhaps out loud. It must have been out loud because Shadow raised his head as if to ask him what was so funny. Scott looked at his friend and asked if he remembered how he got his name? "Hummmm... hmmmm... hmmm" was the expected reply.

When Scott brought his new horse home eight years ago, his name was not Shadow at all. His registered name was 'Bethesda After Dark.' Scott knew he had to find a name fitting the stunning black Morgan. After about the third day of having this adorable black beauty follow Scott so closely that he was 'in his pocket,' Scott realized the obvious name 'my Shadow.' It stuck and so did Shadow.

Soon it was barn lights out for Shadow and his stall mates. Scott settled in for the night and lay in bed

222

thinking how he missed hearing the 'cute as punch' ponies.

Chapter 37

New Yorkers

Riding is one of Scott's favorite disciplines, especially with Shadow. It can be a great training tool and another way get to know your horse. In the saddle you can use your seat and your legs as aids to explain the job to the horse. Working the horse and guiding him through the movements he will need to perform once under harness. This use of seat, legs, reins and voice help prepare both rider and horse for carriage driving. Under harness you lose the control you felt while riding. You only have your reins and voice now to guide a horse that is no longer under you, but in front of you.

For Scott, riding was not only a training tool, but a bonding experience with Shadow. Time to experience the horse and learn the nuances of his movements. Noticing his breathing and how it changes with different gaits and using the heart monitor to learn recovery times after each practice session. Sensing the heat that emanates from his body and the feel of that big heart beating.

Riding was so much easier to prepare for than driving. No carriages or harness to load. Just a saddle, saddle pad, bridle and gone, instant freedom. The trails Scott had cut behind the barn would beckon them onto their green paths and soft footing. They had nearly two miles of trails through the woods, leading them to the hay fields and town roads. The paved roads were never busy with traffic and the shoulders were wide and forgiving. Many of the town roads throughout the mountain were gravel which was the surface of choice for them. These roads were well maintained by the town crew and graded smooth regularly to appease the weekenders that were not accustomed to anything but asphalt. Miles of roads that were barely traveled and seemed like their own private bridle path. These roads available anytime for conditioning or just a leisurely ride or drive. To make these beautiful roads even more enticing, were the long rolling private driveways to the visiting weekender's homes. Owners would openly invite the duo to use them as they pleased. Often commenting that when they arrived for the weekend 'how country' it would look to have hoof prints on the driveway as a welcoming to their getaway homes.

Scott loved the idea of so many well-maintained hilly driveways to use, without having to pay the taxes on them. The more New Yorkers seeing

Scott riding or driving Shadow, the more driveway and field permissions came his way! It was such a beautiful part of the world to live in for many reasons. The rural character of the town, as well as the green fields and old farms. Most of the farms were no longer working farms but served as impressive weekend homes for those needing to escape from the city. For the most part, these 'city folk' were a good addition to the small communities they invaded. They had no interest in subdividing fifty to two-hundred-acre farms, but rather to keep and restore the old barns. They would keep the fields open for their enjoyment as well as the beautiful vistas it provided to their neighbors.

This was a win-win for Scott. Most old farmhouses or estates had mature trees that needed regular maintenance, Monroe Tree to the rescue. Then came the second benefit for Scott, all those beautiful hay fields surrounded by forest. A horseman's delight. He traded mowing paths around the fields for permission to use the trails. Everyone was happy as the owner had immaculately groomed walking or cross-country skiing trails and Scott had miles to travel with Shadow.

One nearby neighbor had a beautiful, level, twenty-acre hay field with a view to the west of the Catskill Mountains and beyond. It was in the center of this field, that Scott made a deal to keep a forty meter by one-hundred-meter dressage area mowed for his use. Just a half mile from home, firm well drained grass footing, a stunning view of the mountains and no taxes, does it get better than that?

A farmer from another town was contracted by the owners to hay the entire field two or three times a year to keep the view open. The field was limed and fertilized annually, so the grass would grow fast and hardily. When the grassy field grew high between cuttings, it would hide his private dressage ring from view of the adjacent town road. Just the little path Scott maintained would lead you to this secret arena, surrounded by fields of green and gardens of clover. This was a great place to live, work and play with horses.

Four times a week the pair would head to their hidden garden. Training was always taken seriously considering their goal, but dressage was to be taken most seriously. For dressage is the basis for everything that will be asked of Shadow. How to carry himself, what to do when and where, to develop his mind and body into a champion.

Countless hours were spent in that grassy dressage court. Working on dance like movements and driving through practice cones until Shadow appeared to be doing it on his own without effort.

A difficult task for both, but they enjoyed the challenge. There are several difficult movements a horse must perform when competing at a high level of combined driving. Two of the hardest to master are the 'collection' and the 'canter departure' under harness.

Cantering is one of Shadow's favorite gaits and the 'departure' done correctly is a beautiful thing to see. The goal would be to change from a trot to a canter in a seamless motion. With a supportive outside rein, a slight inside rein and shifting Shadow's weight back, Scott is setting up this one-horse outboard engine for take-off. Then the cue on the inside rein and a low spoken "canter," and they are off, like a cigarette boat on the water. Shadow extends his front inside leg and elegantly transitions into a canter with his front elevated and his outside hind leg powering them away. This will be practiced over, and over again. Horses learn by repetition, as they cannot reason, they 'associate.' Personally, I think it depends upon the horse!

Chapter 38

Ichabod

When winters came with their snow and cold, training would slow down. Groundwork in the round pen would have to wait, it was now time to ride and condition in the snow, or perhaps play in the snow. When the snow was over ten inches deep, Scott would pull Shadow's shoes off for a while. The footing was soft but deep when riding in the open fields and in the hundred-acre wood. They would often stray from the trails, like most boys do when they are playing.

If the shoes were left on at least one would most likely be lost. The front feet would be delayed while stepping out of the deep snow. The back shoe would then catch the edge of the front shoe and pull it off or loosen it. This was a lesson that had been learned a few times. Imagine walking home on four legs and only two shoes. But not today, as they 'fly' through the snowy fields with white powder splashing into the air all around them. The flurry of snow encircled the duo and as if they were in a cloud of smoke or a dream.

When the cloud cleared, they headed back to the trail. Then eventually back to the barn for a hearty meal and warm blanket for Shadow.

Not all their riding was in the winter. Warm weather riding was much easier on hands and toes! The ease of just bringing a horse, saddle, bridle, hay and water made it a tempting trip to almost anywhere. Scott would ask fellow riders where they rode and was always looking for a new place to experience with Shadow. Perhaps not another 'Midnight Ride,' but interesting spots that were horse friendly.

One such place was The Friends of Rockefeller State Park Reserve in Sleepy Hollow, New York. Built by the Rockefellers and with much of the grandeur of Acadia National Park in Maine, also thanks to the Rockefellers.

There were sixty-five miles of trails with stunning stone bridges creating several loop trails. The best part was that it was only to be used for walking and horse driving or riding. No Bikes! No cars, snowmobiles or mechanized vehicles. The trails were sixteen feet wide with packed gravel and stone surface that provided excellent footing for horses, firm but just enough give.

The trails were lined with hardwood trees, huge oaks, poplar and maples. A perfect habitat for migratory birds as well as year-round winged inhabitants. Between the grooves of trees were fields, streams and wetlands. One of the most ingenious things on the preserve was the grooved cement portion of a trail that was submerged several inches under the outlet of Swan Lake. Mr. Rockefeller had designed this unique feature to offer his horses water without unhitching them while driving. With fresh water slowly moving over the wide crossing it was always a treat to watch the horses stretching down for a cool drink. There were no bad views at the Preserve.

This would be a short break in the man-made stream and then, on through the water to the awaiting pristine bridle path. Occasionally a young horse not accustomed to crossing water would be seen getting their first lesson here. It was a pleasure watching a good horseman or horsewoman properly introducing a green horse to the shallow crossing. Asking for one step at a time, allowing the horse to test the depth. Then giving the reins so the head could lower enough to take a drink. Another step, another relaxing sip. Eventually crossing this scary river and on to dry land. Another horse trained to cross water uneventfully. Well done by both.

One of Scott's favorite trails was called Thirteen Bridges. A two-mile-long path that serpentines over Gory Brook. There were indeed thirteen low arched bridges winding back and forth, making a wonderful view ahead as they trotted deeper into the land of 'Horse Oz.' Cool air from the heavy canopy high above and the absence of understory below provided long breathtaking views. When it seemed impossible to get better, it did. The autumn was beyond words, the view from the saddle priceless. The multitude of tree species brings with it a collage of changing colors. It's said that gardening and landscaping are not unlike painting, this was a work of art.

If the color show were not enough, the Preserve's ground crew would use large tractors mounted with leaf-blowers to clear the paths early each morning. Easy for this horseman to think he had died and gone to Heaven.

Scott planned as many visits as he could to this beautiful wonderland. It was two hours away. His policy was that wherever he went he wanted to spend more hours riding than it took him to drive there. It wasn't a problem at this park, it was getting back to the trailer before dark that was the issue. One ominous day, he definitely got more hours in the saddle than his drive time. Much like the greener pastures in Sweden, these two always want to see what is around the next bend and what the next 'best' scene of the day would be. The further they rode into the massive trail system, the fewer signs there were. By the time they decided to head back to the trailer, every turn looked the same and it seemed they were just circling in a big loop. Flashbacks of their 'midnight ride' were racing through Scott's head and Shadow snorted as if to say, "not again!" It was past his grain and hay time and the trailer was nowhere in sight.

The two wandered for some time as the shadows of the trees got darker and darker. Then they stopped in their tracks as they heard the sound of another horse's hooves. This horse traveling faster and faster as it seemed to get closer. The light of the day was nearly gone as they watched this rider emerge from behind them and heading towards them at great speed. A dark horse with a caped rider who appeared to be leaning over like a jockey would do. Neither of them took a breath as the lone rider came into sight, this black horse with a rider who was headless! Then almost like a whisper, the horseman uttered "follow my shadow."

Stunned by what they thought they had seen and heard they turned to follow. As soon as they did the horseman slowed down so they could keep up... but not too close! Before long they started to see the directional signs and then Gory Brook. Scott stopped to let Shadow have a drink while he collected his wits, remembering they were in fact in Sleepy Hollow, anything was possible there. In the distance he could see the next turn of the trail through the brook and the moon coming into view. The moonlight hit the brook like a spotlight and there was the horseman. The magnificent black horse reared up on his hind legs and his front hooves struck out at the fading light. Then off they rode into the darkness, one final command from the horseman, "follow your shadow." Scott did as he said, and still does.

They followed the familiar part of the trail winding over the brook and back to the clearing were the trailer was parked. The parking area empty, as others were wise enough to leave before dark. Scott took the saddle off Shadow's back and loaded it in the trailer along with the blanket and bridle. He gave his trusted black horse a long hard rub on the head and then wrapped his arm around his neck. He whispered, "this is between us, right partner?" "Hmmmmm... hmmmmm... hmmmm" was the expected reply.

Chapter 39

Tappan Zee

It was a while before Scott found the time to go back to Sleepy Hollow. The views and trails were too much to pass up on, but he would keep it to daylight hours next time. He had heard about what was left of the mansion on the Preserve built by Edwin Bartlett and it intrigued him. Erected around 1848, this English gothic style castle had over two hundred rooms. Named Rockwood Mansion, it was built with locally quarried stone and at the time was the second largest private dwelling in the United States. It was one hundred and fifty feet above and five hundred feet back from the Hudson River. The walls were over two feet thick with massive stone. In its day there were seventeen greenhouses on the property that produced grapes, melons, roses and orchids. There was even an electric lighting plant and hay fields to supply feed for the horses. There were six miles of private carriage trails on the property that were sixteen feet wide and had an eight-inch crown in the middle.

The sole purpose of these beautiful trails was to showcase the stunning landscape and gardens to his guests. Although it was razed in 1937, the estates property was leased to and then sold to the State of New York as a park. A perfect place for Scott and Shadow to explore, in daylight!

He planned an early morning ride and much to his surprise when he arrived at the park, there were many other riders unloading. His veterinarian, Mich, was with them, and they all decided to hit the trail together. When the eight horses were saddled the group headed out, with Scott bringing up the rear. It was fun to be part of a group of riders and especially hanging behind a bit to see everything he wanted a second look at, so many things to see. The trail followed along the Hudson River or 'Munneakantuck' as the Native Americans called it, meaning 'river that flows both ways.' Scott studied the river as they rode and tried to figure out how it flowed both ways, puzzling.

Along the river's edge were the remains of an enormous boat house and dock for the coal barge that would supply coal to the Rockwood Mansion. Continuing up the high river bank was a wide plateau cut into the embankment for a railroad bed, still in use today. Remnants are still there where a railway siding was added to supply parking for a private railroad car. Many feet above the railway track plateau was another level of the hillside with the trail they were riding on. One of the best things about the park was that it was still, after all these years, only for walking or running humans and riding or driving horses. No bikes, no motors, drones, metal detectors, camping or open fire. It took you back in time.

Then over the next rise you would look down on the Tappan Zee Bridge crossing the Hudson River in the distance. With everyone's attention on the river and the bridge, they were not prepared for the ground shaking 'whooo-hooooo' of the Amtrak whizzing by below. Several of the horses jumped as well as their riders. Shadow stood resolute, a well-trained 'spook in place' exercise paid off. If Scott didn't flinch, neither would he. He knew what a 'whooo-hooooo' was and must have thought that one hundred feet below them was a good place for it to be.

Once the troop had settled, they moved on closer to the top and the site of Rockwood Hall. That was a thrill, to see the size of the foundation footprint still supported high above the surrounding grade. Still mounted they turned to see the commanding views of the Hudson and the cliffs of the Catskill Mountains beyond to the west. The vista was great, but so was the forethought to share such beauty with anyone willing to make the time. Scott and Shadow were thankful for this wonderful gift.

Scott could have stayed there all day, just enjoying the beauty of nature and professionally landscaped estate. Even after so many years of neglect the mature trees were breathtaking. He thought of how he wished that his tree care business could have had that account back in the day!

Chapter 40

Fortune Cookies

There was much to do to prepare for their upcoming trip to Pratoni del Vivaro, Italy. Scott was thrilled to be chosen for the US Team again and had to start raising funds to help defray some of the cost. A few friends had planned a special dinner with a silent auction to help raise a little money for the trip. There were dozens of donated items including vacation home rentals, paintings by Jackiellen, antique horse books and a sleigh blanket made from a black bear hide. This was sure to summon a large amount or at least some entertainment for the guests.

The dinner was a potluck and there were many dishes to try and many hungry guests to try them. Trays of 'pillows' or more commonly known as manicotti and baskets of garlic knots. Conversation resonated through the room about horses and travel and did Scott know any Italian? He joked how he loved Italian food and red wine, he thought he would fit right in! He was also taking a liking to the bear blanket hanging over a table. The bidding went on and by the end of the evening Scott had won the bear. Happy to be taking it home, but now wondering if he spent more money than was raised.

When desert was set on the tables, Scott did not want any. If it was not chocolate chip cookies or carrot cake, it was not worth eating. Much to his surprise there was a bowl of fortune cookies. How strange he thought to himself at a potluck Italian dinner to have fortune cookies. He took one from the bowl that was being passed around the table and opened it. He dropped the cookie pieces on the table and lifted the small fortune to eye level and read 'He who follows his Shadow will win in Italy.' His eyes widened and he read it again. He had never read a fortune like this, did he imagine what it said, perhaps being hopeful for success?

Priceless was the look on his face, where was my camera then? Bright eyes and big smile and he looked up almost embarrassed when he realized everyone had the same fortune. Everyone was holding them up, laughing and some toasting to Team Shadow's good fortune in Italy.

He looked about the room and caught the eye of the culprit, her smile gave her away. It was a perfect send off and a genuine wish for victory to my two favorite boys, Scott and Shadow.

As for the bear rug, it proudly hung in the tack room near Shadow's stall for a few years and now is the first thing Scott steps on when he gets out of bed in the morning. It reminds him of Shadow and of course, Chinese food. Well, perhaps not the Chinese food... just his good fortune.

Chapter 41

The Road to Italy

This was to be the most memorable World's Single Championship (WSC) for Scott and Shadow. Memorable it was. It all started the same way, loading Judge Manning's horse van early in the morning with Billy once again behind the wheel. Out the driveway by 0800 and with only the memories of the fanfare of two years before. When they reached the turn where friends and family had stood with their flags and smiles, Scott replayed it in his head and smiled. Ruth was in Florida playing golf, thanks to all the money she had earned house and dog sitting. She stuffed it all in a Saltine Cracker Tin throughout the summer months and then headed south for the winter.

There were some traffic delays in the city, but they still arrived at JFK by 1100. Familiarity is often welcome, but this was one time that Scott wished things were not as he remembered. The same old Animal Holding Center still standing. The building should have been torn down years ago, but the staff made up for the aging facility. They were just as helpful, kind and professional as they were the last time Shadow was there. Buster, the supervisor, actually remembered Shadow and Scott. He was a short vibrant man and surely one of the few black rodeo cowboys in his youth.

Scott knew the routine and soon the off-loading, check in and waiting game began. After the attending veterinarian approved the paperwork and horses, the Team was off to the freight terminal. That would surely be interesting. He had flashbacks of the Sweden trip. It had started off in high spirits back in 2004. The Team had unloaded all their carriages and gear and were given huge skids that looked more like enormous metal cookie sheets than the normal pallets you would put freight on. They were about six feet by twelve feet in size and moved effortlessly and precisely by the forklifts whirling by. They started loading their carriages on the skids. Packing all their gear and tack on the carriages and under them, to fit it all in like a giant jig-saw puzzle. They were about half of the way through packing when a Union Supervisor arrived and reprimanded the gentleman who let them start the packing process. The supervisor promptly threw the entire Team out of the building. It had been an awkward experience and left them all a feeling that things were not finished and worry of what to expect when they got to Sweden

This time however, the Team members were assigned two of the huge skids and were able to pack their carriages and gear from beginning to end. Then they watched as the enormous 'cookie sheets' holding everything they would need in Italy were wrapped with multiple layers of shrink wrap. A thick netting was put over each skid as an extra protective coating. Scott was glad to have been able to finish the packing this time and he had a good feeling about the trip. He hoped that his fortune cookie would in fact come true.

After the freight was secured, they headed to the passenger terminal, glad to be minus the huge suitcase that had cost so much extra on the last trip! Scott had managed to stow it on the pallet this time. All he had was his carry-on bag. No apples in it this time, he figured he would surely not make it through security with them again.

This time he left a large hay bag at the Animal Holding Center with Shadow. In the top of the bag was horse tack and a couple horse blankets. However, beneath that, a few flakes of hay from home and a large bag of apples for all horses to share. He hoped the stowed surprise would not be discovered and would be loaded with Shadow for the flight.

Once they had checked in, they headed back to the Animal Holding Center and by late afternoon the horse loading process started. From stall to air box, to trailer on the tarmac, to plane. This time no one was allowed to be in the air boxes as they were loaded on the plane. They could not see the horses until they had checked in at the gate with all the regular passengers. They walked to the back off the plane and the last row of seats were reserved for them. After a brief meeting with the head groom, he unlocked the door and allowed them to see the horses.

The hay bag with the hidden hay and apples was sitting in the manger in Shadow's airbox and that so familiar "hmmmmm... hmmmmm... hmmmmm..." and those big soft eyes. Shadow knew what was in the bag.

The flight was smooth and many trips back to check the horses offering them water and of course a share of the apples. Shadow shared an air box with a stunning big grey horse, and it was a full-time job keeping the hay net they shared full. The hay net was secured between the two horses at their head level. Upon first glance, the black and grey geldings seemed to be playing tether ball. One would snatch a mouthful of hay and pull the hay bag towards themselves. When they started to chew, the bag would swing loose and away towards the other, who did the same. Back and forth it swung all the way to Amsterdam.

Chapter 42

Horseshoes

All Scott's experiences had prepared him to be here on this mountain overlooking Rome. A beautiful city in Italy, a place to be shared with the one you love. He cannot help but think about being home, sitting at his window table overlooking Casco Bay and sharing a bottle of Cellar Door, Cantina Rosa. The lobster boats coming and going and conversation about the day. All the stories he would have to share about his adventures. For now, with Shadow is where he belongs, it was just nice to know he had a good home to go back to. He took out his wallet and looked at the picture of his family. The smile on Jackiellen and Kate's faces reminded him of another girl with just as wide a smile.

Winter made it hard to train horses in the northeast, so one winter Scott boarded Shadow at a barn in Massachusetts that had an indoor riding arena. It was hard to find a place that would allow drivers to use their indoor facilities. It seemed that most people who rode were leery of having drivers and their carriages practicing around them. Maybe because it is not familiar to them, or perhaps they worried that the noise or commotion would spook their horses. They may not have realized that every experience you provide to your horse adds to their development, especially when they are young. This barn, however, did allow driving and except for the two-hour drive it took to get there, it was clean and warm and allowed for winter training without the snow.

There was a little girl around ten years old that frequented the barn with her mother and watched Shadow's career intently. She was intrigued with the art of driving and was taken with this magnificent black horse. One day Scott asked her if she would like to drive and the wide-eyed girl jumped at the chance. So, Scott had her sit in the driver's seat while he held the reins as well. Off they went together, and the smile was as big as he had ever seen. He had not thought of this young girl or the time he let her 'drive' in years. It often amazes him the ability of a horse to touch us on the inside. Shadow had done this to so many in such a few short years. Scott knew he could never hope to affect people the way Shadow had. It was certainly one of his ambitions to promote positive impressions and encouragement to as many drivers as possible. Following Shadow was difficult, and those horseshoes are hard to fill.

When he thought of filling Shadow's shoes it reminded him of a shoe he had given away. One of Shadow's shoes that he had given a good friend after they had competed on the United States Equestrian Team in Sweden. His friend, starting a new life with her daughters, hung the shoe in her home and ironically it followed her to Portland, Maine. Now it sits on the mantle inside the door of our condo. Years of luck and good wishes and the only time Scott ever gave one of Shadow's shoes away. Perhaps Shadow's blessing on all who enter and all who reside there.

The question has always been, do you hang a horseshoe so that the heel is facing up and catches all the luck that flows into it and does not drain out. Others say the heels should be pointing down, so the good luck falls on anyone passing through the doorway. The biggest requirement is, that it is a used horseshoe not a new one! Pointed up or down, it still brings the spirit of an equine into your home, and that is all that matters. If you are truly fortunate, it will bring a cowboy into your home as well.

Chapter 43

Cream & Sugar

Shadow was settling in after the long trip, horses usually take a few days to hit a low and realize the effects of the jet lag and new surroundings. "Hummm...hmmmm...hmmmm...hmmmm" from Shadow, hoping it is 5pm and time for his grain. Shadow's internal alarm clock makes Scott laugh and think of the little corgi back at home and her "bouf-bouf-bouf" that starts exactly at 5 o'clock, his furry comrades with similar traits.

The Team was training in Milan at Stable de Paciarino, owned by a friend of Chester the Team Coach. The scenery was beautiful and the weather sunny and warm.

Early the next morning, a woman working at the farm was heading out to bring some horses in and asked Scott and Sterling (a fellow teammate) if they would like to give a hand. Eager to help and to see more of the beautiful countryside, they piled into her tiny car. Off they went to a small field some distance away. She pointed to a couple of horses, gave them both halters and said you can walk them or ride them back to the barn, whichever you like. Sterling said mischievously, "we will ride them." So off they went to climb on these tall and tough steeds with no saddle and just a halter and lead line. When Scott grabbed the mane and swung a leg up and over this tall steed, he thought of how the Indians had made it look so easy in the old westerns. It was certainly no gymnastic movement to behold, but at least he made it up without continuing off the other side. Once straddling this high broad back, he reminded himself that this was no Shadow!

They headed back weaving narrow roads around houses and people, then Sterling said, "Not bad for a couple of Lipizzaner stallions?" Scott was horrified, he hadn't thought to check, thinking they were geldings. Halfway around the world and he was going to die on a crazy stallion. He knew it was a bad idea to ride a strange horse bare back, let alone through a village, but this made it even worse. Never was he so glad when his feet hit the ground...and on his own accord!

The next day things got much scarier, and suddenly the stallion story was nothing. Shadow was sick, his vitals were all over the place. It was a long trip from Schiphol Airport in Amsterdam to Milan, Italy, over one thousand kilometers that took twelve hours. The horse van Shadow was in had poor ventilation and some of the hay was moldy. Scott also questioned the horse stop-over in Luxembourg. The stall walls and straw bedding were not clean, and you know how Shadow hates straw! It took a couple days to set it, but it was a form of respiratory infection and was quite serious. The farm's veterinarian knew very little English, but Scott made it clear that they needed to be very careful what medicine they gave Shadow. All possibilities of treatment must be looked at. USEF rules are very strict on what you can give a horse within so many days of a competition, and the horses could be tested for drugs at any time on the showgrounds. It would not matter if a drug was medically helping the horse or not, they would be at risk of elimination. The same way athletes are tested at the Olympics.

Chester was very helpful and called his veterinarian in the States. He obtained the correct information about what type of injectable drug would not only cure Shadow but was an authorized substance. Chester's veterinarian also prescribed starting Shadow on IV drip of fructose and sucrose. The attending veterinarian depleted his supply of the IV solution and went off to get more. They call it a drip IV, but it seemed that the solution was running more like a river. They went through countless bags until a change was noticed in Shadow and he was passing urine. That may not seem to be a sight that one would take pleasure in, but it was.

A catheter was put in Shadow's neck and Scott stayed in the barn from that afternoon until late the next morning changing the IV bags every thirty to forty minutes. It was a long night with a positive outcome and proof that 'the solution to pollution is dilution.' Also, a true testament to the Morgan breed, tough as nails!

If it is not your own hay, inspect it carefully, lesson learned. Second lesson learned, when using a multi-horse trailer with poor ventilation, don't let your horse be loaded first, because of limited air movement.

When Shadow was well enough, training resumed. They only had a few days left before moving to the competition grounds in Pratoni del Vivaro and had lots of work to do. Cones were on the agenda and the day had been a success, so Scott headed off with Shadow for his 'after work walk.' They followed the cobble stone road and took in the beautiful scenery. There were fields of crops and pastures of horses. Tractors here and there carrying out their assigned chores and an occasional bicycle.

About a mile from the farm, they came upon a herd of cattle grazing. They came closer to the fencing as Scott and Shadow passed as if hoping they had more hay for them or were there for a visit. Shadow looked at the cows coming closer and studied them for a minute. He took a couple big sniffs and glanced at Scott with a mischievous eye and lowered his head and plodded along. Scott knew what was going on in Shadow's mind. He remembered the time he took Shadow to a farm in upstate New York where a friend practiced reining and roping. Scott had been dabbling in roping and had wanted to try reining and cutting cattle. He thought it would not only be fun, but a great thing to have Shadow experience being in and around the cows as they had not been before. Sometimes the unknown is scary, so he jumped at the chance to try his hand at it.

When they arrived and saddled up, they entered a pen about 200' by 600' in size that was surrounded by grey galvanized metal fencing. There were about fifteen head of steer in the pen and they were a mix of colors. Some may have been Herefords; it seems that this Cowboy can identify a horse a lot better than identifying a cow.

Here was Scott, thinking he was exposing Shadow to something new and exciting and worried how his horse would do. He should have worried about himself! Shadow was a natural, plowing into the midst of the cows and instinctively driving the exact cow that Scott had intended to cut from the herd. The pair had an amazing time with these fellow cowboys, and they practiced cutting out cattle over and over again. Another notch on Shadow's saddle and exposure to what was foreign to him.

Scott laughed and asked Shadow if he missed 'his cows'? Who knew that when you are in Amish country getting harness you need to buy lawn cows? Some people have fountains or flamingos, but Scott thought 'perfect' some cows for his horses to get used to and he had no idea how much fun he would really have with this herd of bovine.

He bought three of them, all three were black and white with horns, Holsteins, and Scott was slowly learning cow breeds. One was lying down, one standing grazing and one walking with her head up and all life-size fiberglass replicas. Conveniently another customer, perhaps buying flamingos or wishing wells, was trucking his lawn ornaments home and agreed to meet Scott in Newburg, New York, with the cows in tow. This saved more than half the travel distance for Scott with his flatbed dually truck. The two men could carry the heavy cows one at a time very awkwardly. One grabbed the head and one grabbed the tail and they managed to get them loaded on the flatbed. But that was not enough for Scott, he had to line them up tallest to shortest and all facing the passing lane. For the two-hour drive home Scott entertained all the late commuters on the road that evening. From young children waving at the cows to truckers blowing their horns to concerned citizens wondering how it was legal to ship cows in this manner and should they call 911? Would they ever give milk again?

Now at home with his new herd of cows, he unloaded them with his tractor equipped with forks. After placing them in the field, Teton, Shadow's nephew, got the courage to go over and smell the tallest one that appeared to be walking towards him. One sniff and a slight nudge with his nose and the cow went flat on its side. Teton bolted in the opposite direction in horror. Once composed, he walked back confidently thinking he had just laid out this ferocious creature to protect the rest of the animals with one toss of his head. Shadow chuckled to himself. He knew what a cow was, heck he had cut some out of a herd, this was no cow!

Scott was very happy with the outcome so far. He entertained Interstate 84 and had caused quite a commotion with the horses but now the real fun started. Many of the neighbors were weekenders from New York, so they would come and go and often slow down on the way by to see what activities were going on with the horses. Now they saw three cows, with horns in the paddock with the horses. Everyone thought they were real.

From the road they had the right form and size. To confuse everyone more, Scott started a Sunday evening roundup ritual. Using the tractor, he would move the cows around to different positions in the field. That clinched it. The cows were real. They may still be there today as they stayed with the property, maybe they still are being moved around perpetuating the illusion or maybe they have grass growing up around their knees.

Chapter 44

Now That's Italian

Scott was very thankful that the Shadow crisis was over, and he was nearly back to normal. He got in his ugly green Volkswagen Passat stick shift rental car and headed to the Leonardo da Vinci Airport in Fiumicino, the International Airport into Rome.

He was going to pick up the rest of Team Shadow which consisted of his trusted navigator Sue Mallery and Tracy Moran who he hired to be a groom. As groom, Tracy would see to all of Shadow's needs while Sue and Scott walked the course and attended mandatory meetings. Scott was hoping that their plane would be on time as he had special plans for their welcoming. This would be just about the only night to relax before moving to the event grounds in Pratoni del Vivaro. The only night before the tension of the competition would take over and the first night, he could let his guard down, knowing Shadow was going to be all right.

He had many stories to tell Sue and Tracy already and the competition had not even started yet.

Enrico Paciarino owned the stable where they had set up training camp. Enrico had mentioned that he had a restaurant in a little villa called Fiano Romano just outside of Rome and insisted that they try it. Scott and Italian food...yeah that took about a second to decide!

Sue and Tracy's plane arrived and as soon as the baggage was claimed they headed off to find the little villa and the restaurant called 'Paciarino's.' It was real deal Italian. The large beautifully decorated room looked like it fell out of the Godfather movie. Everything was homemade, and the wine was overflowing. They had a selection of bottled wine and fresh young wine that was served chilled. There were kegs of the new wine and they served it in big pitchers that were set right on the tables as soon as you sat down. You don't get a glass of water on your table that quickly in the United States. There were no preservatives in the young wine, and you could drink to your hearts content with few ill effects in the morning. It tasted like a red blend but was light and refreshing and would pair well with any dish. He knew someone at home that would love it and toasted her as always.

At dinner the three were amazed with a new dish that was as much fun to watch being prepared as it was to eat. The chef came out with a rolling cart to prepare a dish for the table right next to them. On the cart was a huge wheel of cheese, hollowed out in the center to form a large bowl. A bottle of whiskey was opened and quickly ladled into the bowl. The chef nimbly lit the flammable liquid. It burned in the 'cheese bowl' while he delicately scraped the sides of the bowl to loosen some cheese. It must have been a Parmesan or Romano by the wonderful smell. Sauce covered noodles were poured into the large bowl of cheese and the chef stirred them around with a big spoon pulling more of the molten cheese into the steaming and aromatic delight. Scott quickly changed his order!

While they waited for their servings of the mouthwatering creation, conversation picked up with a family visiting from The Netherlands. US politics was brought up and dropped again as soon as Scott could manage to change the subject. Politics, religion and the great pumpkin were topics that are best to avoid. So as soon as it was possible, the discussion was turned to sports and horses, a nice common ground.

Their new friends asked how they got horses to Europe. Scott told them about the 'flying horse' and how the process worked. When he mentioned flying in and out of Amsterdam, they suggested visiting The Hague and of course, Louwman's Auto

Museum. Since Scott had already visited the auto museum, these Americans now needed to see 'Deltawerken.' With a wonderful meal, bountiful wine and new Dutch friends they started the sixty-mile trek to training camp.

Chapter 45

Jiggity Jog

0500 finds Scott making a quick call home and then off to collect Sue and Tracy and head to the grounds.

Scott found the cards that were packed in his suitcase. Surprises from home and a tradition he had started, usually hiding a card for each day he would be gone. The cards would be found next to her favorite tea, or in the fridge next to the orange juice or maybe under a place mat on their table by the window. For her, there was only luggage to hide them in, tucked into a blazer pocket or in his boots perhaps. This was a special card by Pamela, an illustrator who she had met a few years before at a Children's Literature Festival in Vermont. The style and subtle inclusion of bees, whales and crowns in her illustrations made an incomparable collection of greeting cards with sentiments just as striking. This one simply said, 'Be the Black Horse.' Three English pennies were inside.

It was very hard to find an English Pound to send on the trip for luck, like the one he carried so many years before. It was his way to remember the amount of contact one should use when driving a horse. Not so much the actual weight, the coin was more of a mental reminder of lightness. One of his favorite mentors, Lisa Singer had taught him you only need a pound of contact on the reins if your horse was trained correctly. Unfortunately, the original coin was lost, but often mentioned.

On a recent visit to Maine Gold & Silver looking for such a coin, a kindly gentleman reported he did not have one. Curious of the reason for seeking the coin and interested to hear about Scott and Shadow, a compromise was reached. He quickly looked up the weight of the coin and what would be the equivalent. It seems an English penny was very close in weight and he appeared with a box full of old coins. Searching through the box he found one with Queen Elizabeth's grandfather, then one with her father and then one with her. The whole family.

When I asked the cost, he put them in a small bag and simply said "tell them Good Luck." That was that. It seemed wrong to look further for a specific coin when this man had been so kind to spend the time looking and to give this token to wish Team Shadow well!

All hands were on deck at 7 a.m. to prepare for the horse inspection jog out. Most people refer to a Combined Driving Event (CDE) as having three phases: Dressage, Marathon and Cones. Scott would argue that there are five phases. He would add the Horse Inspection and the Veterinarian check before Cones. Each of these additional phases is just as important and failing either one can eliminate you from the competition altogether. The purpose of both inspections is for the officials to see your horse is fit and sound to compete. This sport's foundation is all about the welfare of the horse, as it should be.

The team members were at their appointed stations and preparing for this first important event. Tracy were busy grooming Shadow and Sue braiding his mane with black yarn to accentuate his strong and handsome neck. Scott was going over all the harness and carriage with the white glove test, so they were ready for dressage later in the day. Scott supported the traditional attire for the United States at such an event. The entire Team were wearing tan trousers, navy jackets and white shirts with splashes of red throughout their ties and scarves, uniformly projecting the colors of the United States.

As always, Scott would jog Shadow out to be inspected by the officials and had to look his best.

The jog out went well, and some comments were made that it was hard to believe that Shadow, a Morgan, was holding his own among the Warmbloods of Europe. Shadow snickered to himself, thinking that he had as much grit and talent as any horse and wondered what all the fuss had been about. Phase One ended successfully, and like another huge family dinner that took hours in shopping and planning, it is over in literally one minute. Scott was proud to see the stunning Morgan jog out in front of these World Level Officials, an honor most people never receive. One more great memory for Shadow with his dedicated team behind him all the way.

No more time to think about it now, back to base camp to change out of nice clothes and head out to walk the marathon obstacles for a few hours before preparing for Dressage that afternoon.

Chapter 46

The Statue

The Marathon had eight obstacles and within each obstacle there were six gates to maneuver in the correct order at high speed. The distance between each of the obstacles added up to approximately 10 kilometers, or six miles. This made walking the course very time consuming if you are on foot. During many of the events in the United States, competitors can use four wheelers or golf carts between the obstacles to save time and energy. In Europe, however, it was on foot or on bicycle, so they rented bikes and headed out on the course.

The course was set up in the old style with long distances between obstacles. The terrain was very hilly, to challenge the fitness of the horse. It also challenged the fitness of the driver and navigator and their ability to get to each obstacle several times to memorize patterns and organize their time and speed. Unlike today's courses, all the obstacles were not visible from one location. It was truly an 'obstacle course' and they would need to be on top of their game.

Knowing they would have to bike several miles each day, Scott and Sue had started biking at home weeks before to get conditioned for the hills and distances. However, riding a bike on paved or dirt roads at home was no comparison to the hilly grass trails here in Italy.

Needless to say, they peddled some of the way and ended up walking the bikes up the steepest terrain. This gave them an indication of what a horse had to endure during the event. They would be sure to work in short rest periods at the walk for Shadow, wherever the trails would permit between obstacles. Soon their time was up, and they were headed back to base camp to prepare for Dressage.

Scott tried to treat this like any other warm up, not letting the glitz of a World Competition affect him or Shadow. Most would hope things would go well and they would try to not be intimidated by the European Warmbloods. Scott's attitude toward the competition was "I don't think about them, let them worry about me & Shadow."

Shadow was forward, energetic and consistent in his movements, but compared to some of the Warmbloods, a Morgan can look dull. Every breed has is pluses and minuses and there is always a tradeoff. The Warmbloods were excellent in Dressage and were bred to perform, but often their marathons are weak. Much of their movement is up and not forward. This makes a beautiful dressage mover but may make them a slower competitor when it comes to speed, strength and distance.

Scott was hoping to get an acceptable dressage score and to move ahead of the pack in their marathon performance and cones. One of great things about this sport is that it challenges competitors and their horses in three different ways which are all foundationally connected. It is very rare to see a horse that can bring all three attributes to the table. Dressage is the connecting link between the three phases of the competition. The link that takes the competitor to their highest level and horses to the edge of their limits. Fitness, stamina and strength coupled with dressage is what wins obstacles and consequently wins marathons. Shadow was the perfect example. He is powerful and responsive in his hind quarters, supple and engaged in turns and light in his front...what could be better?

Soon they were on deck and with game faces on they entered the arena. Shadow's immobility at the halt and initial salute were perfect, you would have thought he was a statue. There are five judges scoring at this level of competition, so there would be no hiding mistakes. Removing his hat to salute, then signaling his statue to move forward, the test began. The more obedient and willing your horse appears to do the job required of him, the better the score you could receive. Each of the eighteen movements would receive a score of 0-10 from each of the five judges.

The ten-meter collected circle done at a trot using one hand was probably the most difficult. Once the first circle was finished you had to change direction to make a ten-meter collected circle the other way to ultimately form a figure eight and then transition into an extended trot. Scott and Shadow traveled the pattern in unison and as usual Sue was invisible. They tuned out everything around them to concentrate on the task at hand.

The final salute to the head judge and out of the arena and when breaking the line of the gate, they drove back into the world around them. They checked the results of their dressage test and began preparing for the rest of the competition.

Once a competitor leaves the arena, the score sheets are collected, and the raw scores are used to formulate the final score. It is much more complicated, but this is the simplified version. Each judge can score each movement from one to ten, the higher the better. At the bottom of the scoresheet, there are also scores for General

Impressions. The formula totals all the points given to a competitor and then divides it by the number of judges. This figure is then factored by the coefficient used for the appropriate level of driving which is printed on the bottom of the score sheet.

Then any penalties accrued would be added to the score. Penalties could be assessed for things like dropping a whip, use of bandages or protective boots covering a leg or foot of the horse, disobedience of the horse, or grooms speaking, handling the reins or dismounting. There are many more, and hopefully none of them would be cited today.

The lowest score would be victorious, Scott and Shadow received a 49. Not the best dressage test they had completed, but certainly not the worst. They were awarded for 'Outstanding Dressage' for being in the top twenty-five percent of the scores given. Not a bad start to the competition, Team Shadow was pleased.

Chapter 47

Ankles

Dressage over, Scott and Sue headed back out on their 'bike-athon' over hill and dale. The soreness in their legs made it hard to believe they had conditioned at all. That may have led to Sue's loss of balance coasting down a rough hill between obstacles that ended with her in a heap at the bottom and the bike in a heap in the trees. Unfortunately, not only her pride was injured, but also her right ankle.

Once the long walk back to base camp was over the icing process began. Scott had suffered several sprained ankles over his years of sports and knew the protocol well. He also knew that if recovery was not fast, a substitution would have to be made. Half way around the world, during a world level competition was not the time to be looking for a new navigator. Sue and Tracy would have to switch roles. Although Tracy was an accomplished rider and had spent some time navigating, she was no replacement for his 'tried and true Sue.'

Up until now, Tracy had not been allowed to walk the obstacles, as only the driver and navigator can go through them during a competition. Fortunately, Sue's rental bike was in good condition, barring a few dents and nicks. So as soon as they had Sue stocked up with plenty of ice, Tracy and Scott went out on course. They would have to walk each obstacle countless times to memorize their route and know each other's job every foot of the way. If you walk the obstacles so many times you are bored with them, it will become 'muscle memory' and that is the trick.

These obstacles would be particularly difficult to maneuver through, they should be as this was a world level event. Some obstacles were considered short, meaning gates 'A' through 'F' were located close to each other. Other obstacles were long, possibly having the 'A' gate on the opposite end of the obstacle from the exit gate. All the other gates spread out in a maze. Quite often obstacles would be set up on a hillside making if difficult and dangerous to maneuver at a high rate of speed.

Nothing they threw at Team Shadow was really new to them, they had completed many challenging courses over the years. It was the structures, the immovable rigid objects, built at each turn that could intimidate a driver. Knowing that if they nicked one of these corners when flying around a turn, it could easily up-end the horse and carriage in the blink of an eye.

One obstacle in particular, #6 was not only interesting but also daunting, because the best approach to the 'A' gate was along a side hill. This approach would be several meters shorter than the flatter and safer route that many would take. This would help give Team Shadow an edge and a faster time to the end gate. Think of the marble in a roulette wheel spinning along the curved side waiting to drop into the winning slot. Shadow would have to go fast enough along the slanted 'roulette' hillside to stick to it, preventing them from rolling over, because gravity would want to have its way with them. Gravity lost, at least this time.

Scott thought the worst of the obstacle was over and he was pleased that they had challenged themselves and succeeded, once again pushing the envelope. Driving over the steep rolling mounds of earth seemed much like skiing through moguls down a slope. The course designer had done a great job making driver, navigator and horse think of their limitations while getting through all the gates as fast as possible. One way to see how dangerous an obstacle could be was to watch how many spectators would stay at that location all day. Not unlike

NASCAR, everyone wants the thrill of the speed and risk each driver takes on every corner.

Up to this point, Shadow had done very well by remaining among the top three of the fastest times. Then came the fatal mistake, gate 'D' was positioned at the peak of a small mound that made the right turn into it precarious. Having walked it so many times Scott was confident he, Shadow and Tracy would do exactly what they had planned. This turn, every turn, in every obstacle was a well-choreographed dance, rehearsed on foot to the point that it would be automatic once Shadow was brought into the mix. Their run through every obstacle would look fluid, effortless and the hardest thing to do... 'make it look easy.' Not today, not this obstacle, not this time. For whatever reason, Tracy leaned to the outside instead of the inside of the carriage on this tight turn. Rather than keeping her weight inside and forcing the inside rear wheel to stay connected to the ground, she leaned outboard and let gravity do the rest.

As Shadow was halfway around the turn, Scott felt weightless and helpless for a brief moment which seemed to play out in slow motion. He knew what was happening, while not wanting to believe it possible. Somehow through his great strength, Shadow did not allow the overturned carriage to pull him to the ground as well. Tracy flew clear of the carriage, but Scott tried to stay with the ship, holding onto the reins. Never let go of the reins and a flashback of the stone wall, overturned carriage and his beloved black horse running away filled his mind. Not today. He would not let go of the reins.

As with all world events, the other US Team members try to follow their Teammates from obstacle to obstacle cheering them on. Luckily this was the case in Obstacle #6 on this day. It seemed no sooner than the carriage hit the ground, that Scott and Shadow were surrounded by red, white and blue, and it wasn't the British!

His left leg was pinned under the carriage, but his pride hurt far worse. He had one of the best, if not the best Marathon horse in the world. Yet here he was looking up at Shadow from the ground, in the middle of an obstacle in the middle of Italy with one hundred spectators watching. A sickening feeling knowing he had let down the US Team and kept Shadow from an individual medal if not a Team medal as well. This was not the time, there would be many a beer to cry over later. The course had to be completed.

The Team members up-righted the carriage. Scott and Tracy took their positions and off they charged to finish the last gates and on to the end gate. There were just two more obstacles to go.

In the kilometers before the next obstacle, Scott's mind was spinning, he was heartsick, mad and disappointed. Focusing on the memorized path through the rest of the marathon was what he knew he had to do. So, for now he was just thankful. What a blessing that Shadow, Tracy and he had not been injured. Somehow through strength and grit, Shadow had prevented the rigid stainless-steel shafts of the carriage from rolling him over alongside the four-hundred-fifty-pound carriage plus Scott's weight. Such an amazing horse.

There was an uncomfortable silence after leaving Obstacle 6. Scott tried not to think of how things could have gone so wrong on a well-prepared turn. Tracy finally broke the silence. In a shaky and apologetic voice, she murmured "I think I caused the accident." Nothing else was said and all three of them went into competition mode when the next obstacles appeared in the distance.

Shadow sailed through both, as if nothing had happened. In Shadow's mind, nothing bad had happened. It was an unscheduled rest stop for him, certainly unusual in the middle of an obstacle with 100 people watching, but a rest, none the less. They crossed the finish line within their allotted window of time, even with the turnover. Scott knew that even making time, the penalty points would hurt. For now, it was all about Shadow and making sure he was injury free. They headed back to camp to undress Shadow, cool and wash him down and examine him. Fortunately, due to the protective leggings that he wore, there was not a scratch on him. Same could be said for Tracy, besides some minor bruises, thanks to her helmet and protective vest, she would be fine.

Scott procceded with several hand walks for Shadow that afternoon to keep him from 'stocking up' caused by lactic acid deposits from the physical exhaustion. This gave the two a long time to talk about the day and for Scott to apologize to Shadow many, many times. With the confident deep soft eyes of the warrior he is, he all but said it was ok. Shadow was sure there would be another World's with Scott.

The scores were posted and having turned over and accruing twenty penalty points, put them far from medaling. All that was left now was to do a respectable cones course and finish their dream of competing on the US Team on the beautiful hills of Italy.

Chapter 48

Croissants

Rocca di Papa was the little village where the Team stayed during the competition. The hotel was located about three miles from event grounds and was a quaint old two-story building with lots of rooms and a restaurant. Very few people spoke English as they were far enough from a large city and not many needed to know our language. The restaurant had a few menus that were printed in English or you could simply point to what you wanted and there was no language barrier. As soon as you sat down, bottles of wine were promptly placed on the table, a welcome companion after the disappointment of the day.

Morning came early and thankfully the hotel served a continental breakfast every morning. Just before Team Shadow would leave at 0500, one of the hotel staff would arrive carrying boxes of huge buttery croissants from a local bakery. The smell of strong coffee and warm croissants filled the air and of course all the butter and jam you could heap onto your plate. A few for the road and off they would head to the grounds and to Shadow.

The order of go for cones is the best go last. So, along with others who accumulated several penalty points, they would be going early. Course designers like to be quite imaginative when it comes to designing a cones course. This one was interesting, but nothing they had not driven before, just laid out in a different order. Shadow sped effortlessly through the cones, leaving all the balls in place, only one of two competitors that day to drive a clear course. The other was the British driver that won the cones, no time or ball faults. Scott had not made the time allowed missing the window by three seconds. Three seconds be damned, he could not have been prouder of Shadow and could not have been happier to have Sue back on the carriage, where he wished she had been the day before. The day ended with the Closing Ceremony which was always a sight to see and the usual lump in Scott's throat would develop when the US Team dawned the field and he carried the American Flag one more time. He thought the greatest memento of the adventure in Italy was the flag. He had brought it with him and had asked all the members of the team to sign it and still flies it today.

It is anticlimactic to be competing for your country and yourself one moment, adrenaline pumping and heart racing and the next minute to be tearing down base camp and packing the trucks to start the journey home. Trading a few shirts, hats and pins with comrades and final handshakes and hugs and it is over.

Hardy Zantke had been the Chef d' Equipe (team manager) for the US Team. He later wrote Scott and told him that he ran the overall scores from all three phases. Without the rollover penalty points, Scott and Shadow would have surely won a gold or silver medal as an individual. Even though it was only a letter, it meant the world to Scott, and that letter was ultimately the greatest memento of his adventure in Italy.

Chapter 49

Hippodrome

The Team Chef d' Equipe had arranged to have all the grooms and navigators taken to the Leonardo da Vinci Airport in Rome. Sue was going home with a limp and Tracy was going home with regret. Scott was sure it would be a long flight for them, but not as long as the drive from Pratoni del Vivaro to Amsterdam. With horses in tow it would take about three days and you always want to have a buffer of time as they only fly horses twice a week and you don't want to miss the flight.

Leaving long before dawn they descended the mountain, weaving down the winding highway that at times had switchback turns. Fifteen miles at a very slow speed with the breathtaking view of Rome with all its lights waiting at the bottom.

The first stop was in Milan, about six hours away and an overnight at Paciarino's Stable and hopefully an Italian meal! Scott drove the Team drivers in his ugly green Passat rental, and it was very slow going as he followed the lorry. All the trucks in Europe had tachographs which automatically record speed and distance. Generally, there must be a half hour of rest for four hours of driving and no more than eleven hours of driving in a twenty-four-hour period. It certainly keeps truck drivers honest and motorist safer, but it makes time pass much slower when you have a long distance to travel.

In a way it made the trip easier, not having to read road maps or translate road signs. Another upside was the ability to enjoy the beautiful countryside, towns and mountains. The downside was when heavy truck traffic separated them occasionally and all the horse vans looked alike. It was sometimes difficult to spot the one that Shadow was in!

Scott's passengers spent most of their time sleeping, until the moments when he had to wake them because the vistas were too spectacular not to share. He wished one of them had been a photographer, what beautiful pictures they could have shared afterwards because the days were clear and sunny.

Enrico was delighted to have the Team back and of course made them a spectacular dish with homemade ravioli smothered in Bolognese sauce. What could be better, well maybe a nice pitcher of fresh red wine, bene!

The next day would be an eight-hour drive to the Hippodrome in France. It was a horse race track, but when there were no races going on, it was used as 'stall, bed & breakfast.' The grounds were nice and lots of grass for the horses to roam and graze. Hundreds of empty stalls lined up as far as you could see, it appeared that they owned the place. There were rooms on the grounds that must have been used by the jockeys and grooms. And as you can imagine Scott's feet hung off the end of the bed, a bit taller than a jockey apparently. Décor was old, the air was stale, and the hot shower was lukewarm. No need for an alarm clock as the resident mice in the walls would wake you at least hourly. The stalls were better than the rooms and Scott thought he should have bunked with Shadow. Hard boiled eggs and cold cuts and lots of white bread for breakfast. Not a croissant to be found. It seemed more like what you would expect for a lunch, but it was fresh, filling and they need not worry about another meal until dinner time.

Chapter 50

Deltawerken

Another early morning as they pulled away from the Hippodrome, each of them with a bag containing a bottle of water, a bottle of Coca-Cola, two hard boiled eggs, an apple and piece of crusty bread. The motherly hostess would not take no for an answer, no soul could leave without a hearty breakfast and a packed lunch.

As the day before, Scott would follow the lorry through the French countryside. Passing signs pointed the way towards many vineyards, wishing he was there with time to spend visiting the beautiful vineyards. For now, he was content seeing so many uniform rows of wine worthy grapes as they passed through each town. 'Winery Jean de Beauvais,' one of his favorites. They produced a lovely Merlot and a very nice Cabernet. Perhaps he would be back this way again, perhaps with his Angel. She was not a wine connoisseur by any means, her idea of red wine is a blend, but he was trying to widen her horizon of wines. Thoughts of home filled his mind and helped absorb some of the six hours it took to get to Schiphol Airport and the Horse Hotel.

Arriving at the Horse Hotel, they were greeted by a tough looking older woman. She looked like an old burlesque dancer who had not removed her makeup yet. She smelled of cigarettes and whiskey, you would not want to meet her in a dark alley.

Not the nicest place they had ever seen, but it offered a little turnout and a chance for the horses to get a break between the truck travel and the flight the next day. Here the horses would have to wait until the airport was ready for them to enter quarantine. The Team and the lorry driver would all get their own tiny dingy room upstairs with one bathroom down the hall to share, but at least they did not hear mice in the walls, though the horses may have.

The next morning Scott called the airport and they had open stalls, so they could bring their horses over to enter quarantine before the evening flight home. Neither horse nor human was sad to leave the Horse Hotel. They loaded up and headed to the airport and soon had the paperwork cleared and horses settled in for the evening flight. These stalls looked like the Hilton compared to the previous night.

They went to the freight terminal to pack all their carriages and gear as they had for the flight from JFK but were turned away. All they were allowed to do was off load their carriages, tack and gear and leave it in a big bay of the terminal. They could only hope things were packed correctly, thinking somethings might never get loaded because they mysteriously disappear. There was no use worrying about what you could not control.

It was still early in the morning and they had several hours to kill before the flight. Now, not allowed to pack and having no chance of seeing the horses until they were on the plane, they decided to do some sightseeing.

Scott had been intrigued by the thought of seeing 'Deltawerken' and asked Sterling if he wanted to go as well. Off they went in the ugly green Passat. As they left Amsterdam, they could see beautiful arched bridges over the canals and the stunning old architecture of the city. The gates were about an hour and a half away and they were curious to see the miraculous work of genius that tamed the North Sea.

Along the way, they marveled at the rows of oyster beds. Canals and waterways with small boats pulling up to local restaurants for brunch. Series of draw bridges up and down the canals as far as one could see. It was so interesting to see how water is held back and then diverted into canals to supply the agriculture and livestock. This elaborate engineering system of gates and damns was called 'Deltawerken' (Delta Works).

They arrived at Neettje Jans in Zeeland, where the Eastern Scheldt Storm Surge Barrier was located. This ingenious system of sixty-two enormous sliding gates was built to prevent another disastrous North Sea flood like the one in 1953. It was a far cry from the depictions of a small child holding her finger in a damn or dyke and saving the town from being flooded.

They stopped for lunch on the way home in a village square that looked like a movie set. If the food, service and scenery from their curbside table was not enough, a line of horse drawn carts and wagons passed by them. Families returning home from the magnificent stone church visible in the distance. What a serendipitous moment, to have traveled halfway around the world for a driving competition and be reminded what driving still means in its simplest form of pleasure and entertainment. They felt they had gone back in time. But the dream ended soon, and it was time to head back to the hustle and bustle of Schiphol

Airport, security lines and the long wait to see the horses.

Chapter 51

No Hoof No Horse

When Scott saw the Air Korean cargo jet, he thought Shadow would be getting the better end of the trip. No passengers, just freight, horses and grooms. If you think 747's look big on the outside, imagine rolling three horse air boxes into the cavernous shell of one. It looked enormous and surely large enough to bring Enrico's restaurant back with him, including the wait staff! This was only the upper deck, packages and mail were in the belly below.

Being a cargo flight meant there would not be a rear row of seating for Scott to sit and easily go in and out to check the horses. Once the horses were secured in their corner of what looked like a warehouse, Scott followed the Captain to his seat. He figured he would be roughing it, so he was pleasantly surprised to find the small but plush accommodations behind the cockpit. A 'cabin' composed of six first class seats and two sleeping berths. The co-pilot stopped to say hello and tell Scott and the other grooms to help themselves to the coolers of sandwiches, snacks, soft drinks and coffee that had been brought aboard for them. As if that wasn't enough, when the pilot was checking that all the cargo was secure, he took to Shadow right away, not a surprise for Scott. Apparently, he had a small ranch and rode western and was fascinated with learning more about combined driving.

Before long he had invited Scott to sit in the cockpit during take-off! This made things even better. He felt a little guilty not staying with Shadow for take-off, but Shadow had become a seasoned flyer. He was no longer the wide-eyed horse, intimidated by flying 36,000 feet above mother earth. He knew the drill. Shadow had his hay bag and Scott was close by to refill it and offer water. Of course, the occasional apple was never refused.

The rules on this flight mandated everyone be strapped in at take-off, so that made it even more enticing to be in the cockpit. It was very different from the days of flying with Dusty in a little Cessna single engine aircraft, going on day hops to Martha's Vineyard and Nantucket Island. The nearby military Huey helicopters reminded Scott of the day Dusty was flying a National Guard helicopter on a regular exercise and took the liberty to change his course.

He landed on the Cornwall Village soccer field to say hello to his neighbors. Fortunately, or unfortunately a photo of him standing next to his chopper appeared in the Lakeville Journal, the local weekly paper. Eventually getting back to his Commanding Officer. Since there was no harm done and Dusty had an outstanding record as a chopper pilot in Vietnam, the matter was dismissed...but not forgotten.

This cockpit was much different, the Captain looked sharp in his uniform, a white shirt with black trousers and a matching flight hat. To Scott's surprise and amusement, once the flight deck door was closed the starched shirts went on hangers, hats on designated holders and their off-duty personalities appeared. The co-pilot donned a t-shirt that sported Richard Petty and his NASCAR #43. The Captain was true to his horsemanship wearing a white t-shirt stating, 'no hoof no horse.' They all got along just fine. The instructions were clear, Scott was to sit in the seat directly behind the Captain and not move or speak until the jet was above 10,000 feet, "aye-aye sir."

Once they reached that altitude, Scott was shown the route on a map and how they would soon be able to switch on auto pilot and enjoy the special deli grinders waiting for them in the coolers.

Another rule was to carry a portable oxygen tank and mask when checking the horses. Unlike the earlier combo flights, there would be no oxygen masks dropping from the ceiling if cabin pressure was lost. Scott asked, "what about the horses?" There was a long silence but no reply.

Perhaps the captain felt he needed to ensure Scott that they were concerned about their breathing cargo below, as he explained his method of decent. When they approached JFK they would start their descent earlier than usual. By dropping altitude further away, the angle for landing was much less severe and less noticeable for the horses, Scott appreciated the early decent as well!

For some reason the rules of everyone strapped in during take-off did not apply to landing. With no objections, Scott headed to the cargo bay and that "hmmmmm...hmmmmm...hmmmmm..." as if to say, "glad to see you and are we there yet?" The landing was smooth just like the captain had promised, but without the insulation in a passenger plane the noise of the engines reversing to stop the giant warehouse on wings was deafening. The last of the apples Scott had stowed away was perfect to take the horses' minds off the noise and rumbling of the landing gear on the tarmac. The taxiing seemed to take forever, maybe because the competition and travel adrenaline was long gone, and fatigue had taken over.

You wonder how many miles of runway there must be to take so long from touchdown to the gate and glad there were not many miles left until they were home again.

The usual last head rub, treats and then blood samples were drawn, then no one could see or touch the horses until they were released from quarantine in three days.

Scott went back up the vertical ladder from the cargo bay to the flight deck to grab his carry-on and both pilots once again looked very professional in the lightly starched white short sleeve shirts with military creases. Scott now understood how pilots always looked perfectly dressed and pressed when they walked off a plane. Hearty handshakes and an invitation to visit the Captain's ranch and they parted ways, never to see each other again. But that was okay, once again the horse brought people together with interesting stories to tell on both sides.

Chapter 52

Straw Horse

Each World's Singles Championship (WSC), seemed to draw more vendors to the show grounds, more spectators more vendors. More spectators were a win-win for the vendors and for the competitors.

One of the many harness makers selling their wares in Italy had harness displayed on a life size fiberglass horse. Scott wondered if it was from the same place that made his herd of cows. A great idea popped into his head, as he headed home. Have a life size horse hitched to one of his antique carriages at his annual fall barn dance.

As Scott's tree care business grew, he had added more barns at his home to store his growing fleet of trucks and equipment. Each painted 'Monroe Green' and immaculately maintained. The main shop was quite large, and the pouring of the concrete floor turned out to look more like smooth granite. Scott enjoyed dancing and thought it would be a nice break for those sick of cocktail parties and longing for an old fashioned 'do-si-do.'

His local small animal veterinarian's wife played the fiddle in a four-piece band, perfect! Myrtle, the fiddle player was a natural. Born and raised on a farm and learned to ride as early as she learned the fiddle. Scott once asked her the difference between the fiddle and the violin, as she played both very well. With a glimmer in her eye she replied, "You will never spill beer on a violin!"

So now where would he come up with a fiberglass horse, the cows would just not cut it. Carl, a neighbor up the road was a very talented art teacher in New York City. One thing led to another and soon Carl volunteered to make a 'straw horse,' larger than life. Two days before the barn dance, they started to ensemble the structure and bring the horse to life. Carl had built a two by four wooden frame as a base to support the chicken wire that he formed into the shape of the horse. He then covered the wire with hay from the haymow and secured it in place with baling twine. The horses watched in amazement while the imposing figure of a large horse ingested bale after bale of their precious hay.

The harness was next, followed by a one-hundred-year-old carriage Scott had restored. Well, he had done most of it, but relied on an Amish friend named Abner Lapp who did a beautiful job of restoring the upholstery and dash, a story for another day.

Shadow was a bit jealous about all the fuss over this imposter wearing his harness and eating his hay. But soon was over it when he got not only his rub from Scott, but dozens of guests to the barn and all the fuss and love he could take.

'Straw Horse' was a hit, along with kegs of beer and a professional square dance caller. Twirling of partners filled the room and once again horses drawing people together, no matter what the horse was made of.

Chapter 53

Because of His Shadow

Team Shadow continued to compete on the East Coast and wrapped up with what would be their last big competition in South Carolina at Katydid Farm. They won their third National Singles Championship there in 2011.

Little did they know this would be their 'Swan Song.' They were selected for the USET Team in 2012 back in Pratoni del Vivaro, Italy. Scott declined, he decided for many reasons, to free lease Shadow to a para-driver he had been working with. A decision he would not regret.

Over the last few years Scott has been working hard to meet all the requirements to be an American Driving Society Official. This seemed like the next step in his driving career. A sport that he knows so well and wants to be part of but in a new way. This path was a long one that was both time consuming and expensive, but worth it. The outcome would give him the opportunity to give back to the sport he loved so much and hopefully share his knowledge and years of experience with other drivers.

His successful competition history as well as years of volunteer work at different events were great help supplying the needed background for this endeavor. Once accepted into the Learner program, he started the task of traveling to different size shows in different regions of the United States and Canada. At each competition he would be a Learner under an **ADS** Official and would be evaluated for his performance. These experiences were amazing and rewarding for him, he learned so many different nuances of the rules and procedures from the 'other side'.

In the past he had only experienced competition as a driver, navigator or coach. Now to approach the same events and the same rules from the perspective of a Judge or Technical Delegate was eye opening and enlightening.

A Technical Delegate is the person responsible for everything at a competition. Everything from the safety of obstacles, roads and tracks, to the number of volunteers, to the amount of water and hay available for horses. They must know all the rules and ensure competitors follow them. They arrive days before a show and work from early morning to late evening making sure everything is prepared and safe. During an event, they are on the move all day, putting out 'fires,' answering questions and making sure everyone knows what to. The TD is the 'go to person.' This is a very important and complicated position and he learned from some of the best like Philip Bateman, Richard Pepin, Holly Pulsifer, Ken Mott, Craig Kellogg and Lauren Reece.

Training in the Learner program gave him a better understanding and appreciation for not only what happens behind the scenes, but why things happen a certain way at a show. What to do when things work perfectly and what to do when things go wrong. There is so much more to an event than what a competitor sees. If the TD does their job correctly, no competitor realizes that anything needed correcting. Scott calls it looking like the 'Duck,' calm on top but legs going like crazy underneath.

Through his experiences learning and becoming an 'r' (recorded) Combined Driving Technical Delegate, he had the opportunity to work with many great officials. It also made him realize his real love was in judging. Which was no surprise to me, I had told him from the start, judging was where he belonged, and I still tease him today!

Having mastered all the phases of a Combined Driving Event (CDE) he was in a good position to judge as he knew what an event should look like and how things should be done. One of his favorite parts of judging is the notes scribed onto each test form. For years he had waited to get his test results after each dressage and studied it intently. Each little remark the judge had made on each movement helped him learn to improve, his homework if you will.

Now he could use his years of experience to give advice to others. His journey to become Combined Driving Judge was long and challenging, but worth it. The opportunity to work with judges like Sem Groenewoud, Ann Marie Turbe' (France), Kail Palmer-Miller, Andrew Counsell (Great Britain), Jiri Kunat (Czechoslovakia), Emma Burge (Great Britain), Debbi Banfield, Marcie Quist, Mickie Bowen, Holly Pulsifer, Boots Wright, Francois Bergeron (Quebec) and John Greenall had been incredible. To get so many different perspectives on how to judge using the same rules is eye opening and an unparalleled experience. He has learned so much and grown as a judge. It is as though his years of training, driving and competing have come full circle.

Today Scott has moved up to an American Driving Society 'R' Combined Driving Judge (CDJ), 'r' Technical Delegate (CDTD), United States

Equestrian Federation 'r' CDJ and 'r' CDTD and an Equestrian Canada Senior CDJ. He is also a Professional Association of Therapeutic Horsemanship International (PATH) Level II driving instructor. He offers clinics and lessons for all levels of drivers and abilities throughout the country and Canada. He also works in a Veterans Equine program at Carlisle Academy in Lyman, Maine. What more could he ask of his career in the world of carriage driving?

All thanks to a stunning black Morgan gelding with big bones, handsome features, good feet, sound mind, strong body, brave heart, with kind and gentle eyes... who once was His Shadow.

Notes

Sometimes our purpose in life is not clear. Scott's years of training and successes with Shadow, although meaningful for him, may have really been in preparation to help others. Through clinics, lessons and coaching he works to improve the relationship and interaction between people and their horses. The horse has the power to heal us from the inside out and give us a source of freedom, power and mobility. A horse can carry or pull you to another place, far away from your worries and cares.

Winston Churchill knew a long time ago that the "outside of a horse is good for the inside of the man." I would like to add, "woman and child" to that.

On May 15, 2015 Scott entrusted Bethesda After Dark, 'Shadow' to someone who needed him more and the story continues. Perhaps someday we will be able to share the next chapters in the life of this amazing horse.

Shadow & Scott Competition Record

1998 Training Level

1st Garden State CDE
1st Gladstone CDE
1st GMHA CDE
1st Laurels at Landhope CDE

1999 Preliminary Level

1st Garden State CDE
2nd Gladstone CDE
1st GMHA CDE
1st Bromont Canada CDE
1st Laurels at Landhope CDE
1st Wethersfield CDE

2000 Advanced Level

8th USET Festival of Champions – Adv. Level
(2nd in Marathon)
1st GMHA CDE
5th Laurens at Landhope CDE (1st in Marathon)

2001 Advanced Level

1st USET Festival of Champions
5th Laurels at Landhope CDE (1st Marathon)
2nd Gladstone CDE (1st Marathon)

2002 Advanced Level

2nd Bromont Canada CDE (1st Marathon)
1st USET Festival of Champions
2rd GMHA CDE
Selected alternate for US Team World
Championship Conty, France
Navigator for Canadian Team World
Championship, Conty, France

2003 Advanced Level

2nd Garden State CDE (1st Marathon)
1st Bromont Canada CDE
3rd Laurels at Landhope (1st Marathon)
1st Gladstone CDE
2nd Fairhill International FEI (1st Marathon)

2004 FEI (Federation Equestrian International) Level

1st Garden State (2nd Marathon)
9th Bromont Canada CDE
12th World Championship Single Horse,
Astorp Sweden
US Team finished 6th

2005 FEI Level

USEF National Combined Driving
Single Horse Champion
USEF Combined Driving Single
Horse of the Year
3rd Laurels at Landhope CDE (2nd Marathon)
1st Gladstone CDE

2006 FEI Level

USEF National Combined Driving
Single Horse Champion
USEF Combined Driving Single
Horse of the Year

American Morgan Horse Association
Competitor of the Year
16th World Championship,
Pratoni del Vivaro, Italy
1st Cedar Lane Farm
1st Garden State CDE
2nd Bromont Canada CDE (1st Marathon)

2007 FEI Level

1st Garden State CDE
1st Laurels at Landhope CDE
1st Gladstone CDE
2nd Bromont Canada CDE

2008 FEI Level

Selected for USET Single Horse Champion,
Poland

2009 FEI Level

1st GMHA CDE
3rd USEF National Championships, Kentucky
Horse Park

2010 FEI Level

1st Sunshine State CDE
2nd Garden State CDE (1st Marathon)
1st Shady Oaks CDE
1st GMHA CDE
Selected for USET Single Championship,
Pratoni Del Vivaro, Italy

2011 FEI Level

USEF National Combined Driving
Single Horse Champion
(first competitor & horse to win three times)
Katydid Farm
1st Shady Oaks CDE

Post Script

To date Carriage Driving in not recognized as an Olympic Sport. Perhaps one day the Olympic Committee will recognize the talent, commitment and ambition of these drivers and their horses.

Currently, Dressage (ridden), Eventing and Jumping are the only disciplines included in the Olympics. We hope for the day that Carriage Driving for para * and able-bodied drivers will be added to the vast array of 'sports' considered Olympic worthy.

Until then, we are thankful for the United States Equestrian Federation (USEF), American Driving Society (ADS), the Federation Equestre Internationale (FEI) and Equestrian Canada (EC). These organizations work together to offer athletes and their horses the opportunity to compete and be successful at a World Level.

*Reference to 'para' here and in this writing refers to a driver with disabilities being parallel or equal to an able-bodied driver. In some cases, perhaps even better than able-bodied drivers.

Bibliography

Carriage Driving
'A Logical Approach through Dressage Training'
Heike Bean and Sarah Blanchard
Copyright 1992, 2004

'Driving the Horse in Harness'
Training and Technique for Pleasure and
Performance
Charles Kellogg
Copyright 1978

'Republican American Newspaper'
Waterbury Journal, Connecticut 2007

'Chronicle of the Horse'
Volume LLXXIII, No. 11
Friday, March 12, 2010

Lolisa Marie Monroe

Author of '*Following My Shadow,*' shares tales of this amazing horse. Her long-standing friendship with Scott Monroe has enabled her to witness and pen the evolution of this dynamic team.

As a single mom she raised two amazing daughters Katelin and Jackiellen to be strong and independent women with great careers.

She was Co-owner and General Manager of Winderosa Manufacturing for 27 years. She changed gears a few years ago due to an illness and moved closer to her daughters.

Lolisa resides in Portland, Maine, with her husband and partner Scott and their corgi Grace.

She currently writes children's books. Her hobbies are photography, working with children and of course all animals.

Photo by Port City Photography LLC.

Made in the USA
Columbia, SC
27 July 2019